Wanted → My First Career

The Definitive Playbook for Landing Your First Job in a Fulfilling Career

Marlo Lyons

Future Forward Publishing

Published in the United States by Future Forward Publishing, Scottsdale, AZ

ISBN: 978-1-7370181-3-1 (print)
ISBN: 978-1-7370181-4-8 (epub)
ISBN: 978-1-7370181-5-5 (audio)

Interior design and production by Dovetail Publishing Services
Editing by Matthew Gilbert
Jacket design by Jeff Zwerner

Dedication

*This book is dedicated to my husband, Brett,
and my children, Macey and Brenner.
You inspire me every day.*

"Just try new things. Don't be afraid. Step out of your comfort zones and soar, all right?"

—Michelle Obama, former First Lady of the United States

Contents

Preface

"The straight line, a respectable optical illusion which
ruins many a man."
—Victor Hugo, French poet, *Les Misérables*

Everyone has a different career journey. What you do with that journey will determine if you are in a job you love or hate. I could have never anticipated my career path when I graduated from college. When I first left home to attend college, I remember my father saying goodbye and reminding me one last time, "College is a time to grow up. The goal is to graduate with a job." So, after graduating from The George Washington University, I knew I had limited time to find a job. Otherwise, I would have to move home and I did *not* want to do that. I was certain that it wouldn't take too long because I did everything I could to prepare for a career as a TV news reporter.

This was in the '90s. I had internships on my resume that included WRC-TV (the NBC affiliate in Washington, DC), CNN, and CBS News Nightwatch where I worked for Lee Cowan, now a CBS News National Correspondent. I also interned for a small start-up production company, Capitol Video, interviewing up-and-coming stars like Flavor Flav, Queen Latifa, and Martin Lawrence in exchange for the videographer helping me create a reporter resume tape. Thirty resumes and videos went out the door. Not one call. I convinced my father the only way I would get a job is if I was in front of news directors. I wanted to drive from DC to Texas and back and interview at every TV station along the way.

At the time there were three affiliates in each market: ABC, NBC, and CBS. I planned to hit all three before leaving each city and prepared myself for three weeks of hardcore job hunting. Every interview ended the same way, either noncommittal or, more often, "You don't have any (or enough) experience." I was even rejected for low-level writer jobs. One Nashville news director said, "Look, someone told me I'd never make it to where I am today and now, well, here I am. You'll get there, just not here." Even though I knew Nashville was too big of a city to break in, I still felt hopeless.

I arrived back in DC with no job and no prospects. But there was a message on my answering machine! "Hi, Marlo, this is Renard Maiuri. I'm the news director at KDRV-TV and I'd like to talk to you about an associate producer role I have in Medford, Oregon." Oregon! My job would be to take prepackaged medical stories provided to TV stations nationwide, rewrite them shorter, have a local doctor record his own voice on them, and then edit the story together. It wasn't a reporting job, but I didn't care. All I knew was I got a job in my field of choice!

Since that first job, I have had nine different careers and more than a dozen jobs. I have been a TV news associate producer; a TV news reporter (including a consumer/investigative reporter) in five states; an operations attorney for an insurance company; an entertainment lawyer managing reality show diligence and production risk at NBC and Viacom (now Paramount); a screenwriter; a movie producer; a career and executive coach; an HR business partner; and an award-winning author! All were completely different careers, though not all of them successful or full-time. Some were "dream jobs" I pursued with vigor. Some were day jobs while I pursued other dreams. I had some traction in each one and each one helped me further figure out who I was and what I wanted. That is my biggest goal for this book: that it helps you figure out who you are, what you want, and how to get it! And once you do get it, you'll learn how to employ my proven *Career Transition Strategies*® to change again throughout your career as you continue to seek personal happiness and career fulfillment. After all, life isn't linear.

Introduction

"Life isn't about finding yourself. Life is about creating yourself."
—George Bernard Shaw, playright

In the journey from high school to college, you might expect a clear path to unfold, guiding you toward the perfect career. However, as I discovered firsthand, the transition to college isn't always straightforward because your classes won't necessarily help you figure out what you want to do or what career will fulfill you long term.

When I was applying for colleges, I had no idea what type of college I wanted to attend, what city I wanted to live in, or what major to pursue. I was a watercolor artist, so my parents suggested I apply to some art programs. I liked watching the news, so my father suggested I consider a political science or journalism major. Being an impressionable teenager long before the internet was commercially used, I applied to a variety of schools—some in the city, some in rural locations, some big, some small, some with sports camaraderie, some with little sports enthusiasm. In the end, I chose The George Washington University. There wasn't any specific reason why I chose that school, so I attribute my decision to my father, who said it was a great school and I'd love it. He wasn't wrong; I did enjoy GW and decided to major in political communication. Despite the prestige associated with my chosen major at the time, I soon realized that it wasn't aligned with my passions or interests. People who majored in political communication wanted to become lobbyists, manage political campaigns, or work on Capitol Hill, none of which interested me.

Nevertheless, armed with my father's mantra of why you go to college—"to get good grades to secure a good job"—I immersed myself in college life. From bustling city streets to the quiet of the quad, I navigated the ebbs and flows of academia, not really thinking about what truly ignited my spirit. Reflecting back on that time, I've come to realize that most of the choices I made before and during college were based on external pressures based on what my parents wanted for me or what I thought was the "right" decision. Some of you may be having the same experience, but hopefully this book will help you rely a bit more on your intuition and align your choices to your values.

Take Jagger, a high school senior, who agonized over her decision between the five schools she was accepted into. Beneath the surface of the choice she faced, Jagger didn't realize she possessed a profound understanding of her core values: a love for nature, a longing for community, and a passion for helping others. Through a simple visualization exercise where Jagger pictured herself waking up and walking to her first class at each college, she immediately uncovered the clarity she needed to make an *intentional* choice—one that resonated deeply with her values and desires. I could hear the relief, happiness, and calm in her voice when she said, "It's obvious what the right choice is for me. I know I would be happy there." And so she committed to her school that night and embarked on a journey fueled by authenticity and purpose, unburdened by the weight of external expectations.

Once in school, the pressure to pick the perfect major or "get good grades" can overshadow the most important part of college: self-discovery. It's common to believe that certain majors are gateways to specific careers, particularly in fields like medicine, where prerequisites are predefined. However, the truth is far more nuanced. For example, if your heart is set on a career in medicine, you might assume that majoring in biology or biological science is the only path forward. The reality is that you can pursue your passion for medicine while majoring in English literature, communications, or foreign languages and utilizing electives to fulfill premed prerequisites. This allows you to pursue your goals *and* explore other areas of interest. Instead of fixating on a specific major, expand your focus to exploring subjects that ignite your curiosity.

Whether you're drawn to literature, technology, psychology, or finance, each major offers valuable insights and skill development for any career. For example, sociology and psychology majors deepen an understanding of human behavior—a valuable skill in any workplace setting. Philosophy majors hone critical thinking and problem-solving skills, essential for navigating complex challenges in any profession. Finance majors sharpen an understanding of business, also a great foundation for any career. Ultimately, the key is to follow your curiosity and seek out experiences that deeply resonate with you. Talk to students and professors in prospective majors, explore course offerings, and embrace being open to learning and growth.

The key takeaway? Your major does not dictate your destiny. No one knows that more than my good friend Julie Goldman. She graduated with a degree in political science, worked for the Congressional Committee for Education, completed two masters in education and even achieved a doctorate in education. "I expected to be the president of a college, but as soon as I worked in admissions for a college, I knew that wasn't my final destination." She moved into entrepreneurship, opening her first business, The Original Runner Company, then selling it nearly two decades later. Now she owns Superfly, a bungee fitness business in New Jersey. "I always enjoyed fitness but thought political science made me look smart. Going into fitness wasn't what my parents would have wanted for me. While I don't regret my path because I learned so much along the way, I wish I was exposed to more in college and tried different things because that is what college should be about. That is what I tell my daughter: 'Try everything, be curious with a growth mindset.'"

I discovered the same thing—the correlation between your major and your future career is often far less significant than you might think. In my own career journey, I have never once been asked about my major, nor has it hindered my success in fields seemingly unrelated to political communication. Contrary to my father's advice, college is not about "getting good grades" or a race to land your first job; it's about discovering who you are and laying the foundation for a fulfilling and meaningful life beyond graduation. It is through this exploration that you'll cultivate knowledge and rich experiences, shaping the person you are destined to become. Your "career" will come in due time, so commit to your passions, embrace the unknown, and, above all, revel in the journey of becoming your most authentic self.

If you are reading this book at the beginning or even the middle of your college experience, you will learn more about yourself by doing these five things:

1. Dedicate yourself to earning a degree in a subject that truly captivates you.

2. Take time to delve deeply into self-exploration. Discover what ignites your passion, what doesn't, and why.

3. Seek internships in various careers across different industries to gain a foundational understanding of the working world.

4. Cultivate meaningful connections both within and beyond the college community; recognize the invaluable role of quality personal relationships in your life.

5. Have fun. Yes, FUN! Prioritize enjoyment and seize every opportunity for fun and fulfillment along the way.

If, on the other hand, you find yourself on the cusp of graduation or have just crossed that milestone, congratulations! I hope you had some fun on your journey of learning and exploration. Your entry into adulthood begins now, and *you* hold the power to shape your own success. Reading this book is the first step!

Be Intentional

"Intentional living is the art of making our own choices before others' choices make us."

—Richie Norton, entrepreneur and author

As the title of this chapter suggests, being intentional is key to navigating your career journey. Throughout college, you're not only exposed to fascinating subjects and diverse perspectives but also afforded the opportunity to discover more about yourself. Understanding your desires and aspirations lays the groundwork for shaping the career you envision. While considerations like a generous salary, remote work flexibility, or ample vacation time may feature prominently, what I have heard from college students is that the desire for engagement and fulfillment in their work resonates most. This chapter serves as the starting point for embarking on a quest to find a career that excites you and aligns with your values, even if you're unsure about your ultimate destination. At its core, it's about embracing intentionality as the catalyst for charting a fulfilling career path.

Tip #1: A fulfilling career starts with intentionality.

Be Intentional in Everything You Do

So, how do you know what career to pursue if you don't know what will be fulfilling? Don't worry! This book will:

1. Guide you in aligning your career with your interests, passions, and values, ensuring fulfillment.

2. Equip you with the tools and confidence to secure your first professional job and gain skills to advance your career.

3. Teach you how to transfer skills from previous work, internship, volunteer, and life experiences to your current or future career path.

When you hear thought leaders describe their careers, it is evident they are driven by aligning their careers to their interests, passions, and values, which has led to fulfillment.

> *"Your job is not just to do what your parents say, what your teachers say, what society says, but to figure out what your heart calling is and be led by that."*
>
> —Oprah Winfrey

> *"When you have a passion for something then you tend to not only be better at it, but you work harder at it too."*
>
> —Vera Wang

> *"Like my friend Warren Buffet, I feel particularly lucky to do something every day that I love to do. He calls it 'tap dancing to work.'"*
>
> —Bill Gates

> *"The best advice I could give anyone is to spend your time working on whatever you are passionate about in life."*
>
> —Richard Branson

> *"It is a luxury to combine passion and contribution. It's also a very clear path to happiness."*
>
> —Sheryl Sandberg

Yeah, they're famous and rich, so of course they love their jobs. But how about normal people? You know, us? Well, here are a few "regular people" who have also focused on their passions, interests, and values to find the same fulfillment:

"I'm excited about the day and what new is going to happen: Who's going to call? What special project is going to walk in? When you meet with a customer who has an idea and there's land and there's nothing on it and 12 months later there's a building, that's exciting. From concept to reality."

—Craig Fishman, Principal and COO,
NES Group (bank design and architecture), Massachusetts

"I love connecting people to resources and sharing information that is valuable to others. When people come to my retreats, I feel fulfilled. It's so rewarding helping people find their own fulfillment and move in the direction they want to go."

—Kristin Graziano, holistic retreat facilitator, Arizona

"When I'm in someone's home and helping a client understand how to style something that makes them feel more confident, bolder, or just happier, I feel like I made a small difference in someone's life because they say they could have never done this for themselves without me and that just makes my heart full."

—Amy Brubaker, personal wardrobe stylist, California

"I love being able to speak to someone who is nervous and tailor their experience by making them feel comfortable mentally, physically, and emotionally with their surgery and confident they will have a great outcome."

—Shelly Gierat, certified registered nurse anesthetist, California

"I love being a hair stylist. I get to build deep relationships with a wide variety of people, so I learn about culture, religion, politics, and food, and I travel the world with them virtually when I hear about their adventures. Most importantly, when I'm done doing my job, they feel good about themselves, and that fulfills me every day."

—Shawn Mahoney, master stylist, Arizona

The previous people found their ideal calling—their perfect career. But not everyone finds it on the first try; some people start in one career and then transition to something else. For example:

> *"I worked in entertainment for more than 15 years, first at an agency, then as a reality producer, and then as a film and television producer. When a movie deal fell apart and investors pulled out, I had to start over and figure out what I was going to do. I decided to become a realtor. It wasn't my passion to start but it quickly became my passion. I am so much happier, so much calmer, so much more sovereign. I still work with some of the same people I used to in entertainment, except now I help them buy and sell homes, and that is incredibly rewarding."*
>
> —Adam Brawer, luxury realtor, California

> *"I am the first entrepreneur in the family and my parents didn't understand why I was taking a risk, leaving a stable, 10-year software engineering career to start a business. But I had a dream of making customers happy by building what they like the most. That was my passion, and I converted that passion into reality. Seventeen years later, I still love my job."*
>
> —Praveen Puranam, owner,
> Custom Creative Remodeling, Arizona

> *"I majored in marketing and started in commercial real estate but knew that wasn't the right fit for me. Now, I am 25 years into teaching, and I love working with the kids. It's amazing to watch them grow and change and when those lightbulbs go off and they say, 'Wait, I get that!' It makes me so proud to see them so proud of themselves. There is nothing more rewarding than that."*
>
> —Sandee Levine, Wilson dyslexia therapist,
> The Jones Gordon School, Arizona

> *"At the worst time of my life, when my kids were in a horrific car accident and my husband was beaten during an armed robbery of*

our jewelry store, a nurse came into the hospital room and said, 'Do what you are passionate about, and it will all come to you.' I said, 'I love to travel,' and 35 years later I am still working as a travel advisor. I live and breathe my job every day and love every minute because I am helping my clients create memories with their families, loved ones, and friends, and you can never take those away."
—Tammy Levent, president, Elite Travel Management
Group Agency, Creator of TASK (Travel Agent Success Kit),
and author of *Sink or Swim*, Florida

"I received a master of arts in professional communication and digital media and immediately fell into my first career as a 12th-grade English teacher because the school needed teachers and I needed a job as I was pregnant with my second child. After five years, I leveraged this experience to move into a tech company which has opened so many doors for me. I am incredibly grateful for this experience, the skills I've gained, and the relationships I've built. And while I love my job, it is just the beginning of my journey. I am now 100% intentional with my career and gaining knowledge every day about our products and AI to eventually become a product marketer."
—Keyana Darling, academy learning manager, Microsoft, Texas

Maintain a Skill Acquisition Mindset

While this book *will* help you find a fulfilling career, your first job out of college does not have to define your entire career path. However, your first job should be approached with intentionality. This means making choices purposefully and with a clear understanding of your values and goals. It's about consciously selecting your first job, being fully aware of the skills you'll develop and how they will serve you in future roles, regardless of what career path(s) you pursue.

Too often, I've seen people stumble into careers they despise or drift from job to job because of happenstance rather than intentionality. *The goal isn't to pressure yourself into finding the perfect career immediately;*

it's about understanding your career desires at each life stage and knowing how to achieve them. Consider the skills you'll gain and their contribution to your growth, even if your next steps are uncertain. This approach will enable you to navigate your career path intentionally with clarity and purpose, ensuring you are ready to excel in any field.

Chapter 1 Summary

1. **Be intentional:** Be intentional about what you want and deserve in your career. Whether you're clear on your goals or seeking clarity, this book is your guide to navigating your path with purpose. Resist external pressures to stray from your aspirations, even when faced with tempting shortcuts or others' agendas. Your first job, like every step in your career journey, should be chosen with intentionality.

2. **Skill acquisition mindset:** Embrace every job opportunity as a chance to acquire new skills. Whether you remain with the same company or venture elsewhere, each role will offer valuable transferable skills that contribute to your career growth. Viewing every experience as a stepping stone enhances your professional development and prepares you for future career moves.

2

Assessing What's Important to You

*"It's not hard to make decisions when you know what
your values are."*

—Roy Disney, co-founder, Walt Disney Company

How many times have you made a list of pros and cons before making an important decision? We may come up with more pros or more cons to skew the choice, but it will still have to be made, and sometimes it will go against what the list seems to say. Don't worry. This chapter won't suggest that you write such a list for various career choices. Those lists are nice, but they don't tell you what you truly need to know. All they reveal is what you like and don't like about your current or prospective position. Instead, take a step back and evaluate more deeply what drives you in life and in the workplace.

Before making any decision, especially one as important as your career, it's best to first identify and understand your values. The Co-Active Training Institute is a professional coach training and certification program that has trained more than 65,000 coaches, including employees in a third of the Fortune 100 companies. Co-Active teaches,

Tip #2: Understand your values to determine what you want in a career.

"Our values serve as a compass pointing out what it means to be true to oneself. When we honor our values on a regular and consistent basis, life is good and fulfilling."[1] Simply put: Making career or life decisions based on external pressures or without identifying and understanding your values could lead to impulsivity, faulty assumptions, and/or setups for failure.

I'm sure you know a few people who jump from one bad relationship to the next. They probably never take the time to think about what is truly important to them, what they want, and what they deserve. They are only interested in getting out of a bad situation or "showing" their last partner that they found something "better." Different isn't always better, though. If you don't keep assessing your core values, you will compare each relationship to the one before it without the wisdom of knowing whether these "significant others" were able to provide something truly important and meaningful. One relationship may seem "better" than the last one but not for long because they aren't filling most or all your core values.

Similarly, I've encountered individuals who have hopped from one unsatisfying job to another solely to escape a negative situation or because they were enticed by the allure of a new title or a higher salary. However, they soon discovered that these superficial career advancements did little to alleviate their dissatisfaction. True fulfillment stems from aligning with one's core values, which include much more than titles and financial incentives. When you prioritize your values and integrate them into your work life, you'll experience genuine happiness, fulfillment, and heightened engagement, ultimately leading to increased productivity and overall employment success.

Values change throughout our lives, so doing a value-identification exercise will provide a helpful snapshot of what they are in a given moment in time. Doing this on your own requires some deep thought and self-awareness, however, so I always recommend working with a coach because they will help you uncover values you may not realize you have or didn't realize were actually values. If hiring a coach isn't an option, I suggest starting with what gives you "energy" or your "likes and dislikes."

Likes and Dislikes

Figuring out what gives you energy starts with asking yourself these four questions:

1. What do I like doing or what gives me energy?
2. What do I hate doing or what depletes my energy?
3. In what kind of environment do I thrive and feel most at ease?
4. What kind of interactions do I enjoy and want to have with others?

Whether you're engaged in work, completing projects at home, or attending classes, dedicate a full week to answering these questions. Pay attention to the emotions and sensations evoked by specific activities or conversations. For instance, you may find joy in researching astronomy but not researching art history. What about research in astronomy is interesting to you and gives you energy? What about art history depletes your energy? Understanding the underlying reasons, or the "why," behind each response is crucial.

Another example: You may prefer intimate one-on-one conversations over group discussions because they feel more personal and meaningful. Conversely, you might dislike large lecture halls because they make you feel unnoticed and insignificant. Documenting these preferences and the associated reasons for and against in a chart, such as the one provided below, can help clarify your values. One of my clients let me share her list of likes and dislikes (this is a partial list):

What do I like? What gives me energy?	What do I dislike? What depletes my energy?
Astronomy class and astronomy research	French history class and homework
Why: I love learning about stars, galaxies, and dreaming about what else is out there.	**Why:** The professor teaches in French even though it's not a French language class and I can't understand him. I hate when I can't understand something.

What do I like? What gives me energy?	What do I dislike? What depletes my energy?
Taking hikes and doing anything outdoors, even when it's hot or raining **Why:** I just feel free and all my stresses melt away.	Sitting for long periods of time **Why:** I feel antsy, like I want to move or get out and "do" something.
Playing piano **Why:** I feel at peace with music. It's active. I love the feeling of the keys under my fingers.	Fraternity parties **Why:** It feels fake when everyone is drunk and I fade away into the background.
One-on-one conversations **Why:** They feel authentic and I can be myself. I don't need a mask.	Large lecture halls **Why:** I feel unseen and unheard.
Working independently **Why:** I like doing work on my own because I like to own things from beginning to end.	People who think they are better than me because they have more money or "status" **Why:** I don't know how to relate to them.
Getting a good grade **Why:** I like being recognized for good work.	Working with people on projects who put in minimal effort **Why:** It's not fair because they get credit for my hard work and don't deserve it.
Knowing what I need to accomplish each day **Why:** I don't like surprises.	Being bored in class **Why:** I feel like I'm not learning.
Meeting new people from different places around the world **Why:** I like learning about different cultures.	People who aren't authentic **Why:** They're selfish and it feels like they will backstab me.
Reading **Why:** I like learning about different things I normally wouldn't learn about.	Messiness **Why:** I feel calmer when things are organized or in some kind of order.

You can also think about your greatest accomplishments in previous jobs, internships, and volunteer activities. Why do these accomplishments stand out to you? If you lack work experience, broaden your scope to encompass all aspects of your life. Reflect on personal milestones that evoke feelings of pride or achievement, independent of external validation. For instance, you might take pride in earning a black belt in tae kwon do due to the discipline and perseverance required, or scoring the winning goal in a soccer game, symbolizing teamwork and dedication. Even smaller victories, like surpassing a personal fitness goal or cultivating a growth mindset, hold significance in shaping your sense of personal success.

Also, consider internal achievements such as overcoming limiting beliefs or embracing your unique strengths and diverse abilities, like ADHD or autism. Recognizing and leveraging these aspects of yourself can contribute to a sense of personal growth and empowerment.

Once you've compiled your list of energizing activities and preferences, delve deeper to identify your core values in relation to work.

Values = What Is Important to You

How do "energy," "likes," and "dislikes" correspond with values? They identify what you feel is important, and once you know that, you can match them with core values. Again, it's easier to work with a coach, but without one, you can google "core values list" to help kick off your thoughts. A more comprehensive list can also be found in "values cards."[2] I'm not a huge fan of these lists or cards because they are limited and won't always represent deeper impulses, but they will get you thinking and that's what is most important.

No matter what method you use, choosing values that truly represent who YOU are at your core is critical. Some people will have twenty values; some will have five. The number doesn't matter; picking *true* values does. Some people will try to be virtuous or pick values they think they *should* have or wish they had. For example, consider the value, "learning new things." Some people love to learn something new. Bill Gates reportedly reads about a book a week![3] Now let's take "John," who is exploring his core values. John admires Bill Gates and wishes he could read and absorb as much information as Gates does. John thus may think that "learning" is one of his core values. He should always want to learn, and he certainly has a desire to, but if John is given a choice between streaming *MrBeast* on YouTube or reading a book, visiting a museum, or watching a documentary, he will choose streaming *MrBeast* every time. While John likes to learn and learning seems like a "good" or "socially acceptable" value, it's not his burning desire or even something he seeks out every day. If John believes that "learning" is a value, he will need to define it clearly to know what that means *to him* because it won't mean the same thing as it means to Bill Gates. It also may not be as important as other values because it isn't something that brings him joy or fulfills him each day.

If you are self-aware enough to stop yourself from choosing values you *want* to have or *wish* you had or that *seem* like the right values to have, you will more easily be able to define those *true* values that will help you make smart decisions about your career and future. From your likes and dislikes, you are now prepared to identify some values. Here's how I converted my client's likes and dislikes list from above into core values:

What I like	Corresponding value
Astronomy class/research	Research
Taking hikes/being outdoors	Freedom; peace
Playing piano	Active work or play
One-on-one conversations	Authenticity
Working independently	Ownership
Getting good grades	Recognition
Knowing what I need to accomplish	Structured work
Meeting new people	Cultural learning
Reading	Learning

What I dislike	Corresponding value
French history class in French	Deep understanding
Sitting for long periods of time	Active work
Fraternity parties	Authenticity
Large lecture halls	Being heard and seen
People who think they are better than me	Humility
People who don't put in effort	Working around passionate people
Being bored in class	Learning
People who aren't authentic	Authenticity
Messiness	Organization
Working with people who are ineffective	Working with smart people

You may be thinking, "Yes, those are my values, too!" But even if we have the same values or likes and dislikes, it doesn't mean they represent the same things. Why? Because each of those words could mean different things to different people. For example, if "flexibility" was one of my values, it would mean that I can attend my kids' school concerts or special activities or end work by 5 p.m. so I can cook a nice family dinner. "Flexibility" to you may mean working remotely. It is therefore critical to dig deeper into what each identified value means to you.

The Co-Active Coaching Toolkit explains how to create a "value string." Use a "stream of consciousness" (unedited brainstorming) approach to write down what comes to mind about each value with a slash between each thought you have about that value. Value strings don't have to be in complete sentences. You aren't striving for perfection here. You are defining what the value means to you with either words or examples. Here are a few value strings:

→ **Research:** I like to dig into a subject that I enjoy / Astronomy is so vast and there are so many different things to learn /

I like to learn about things I know nothing about / When I am researching something I know nothing about, I am hyperfocused and can do it for hours / Research is like uncovering different parts of a puzzle . . . when I have all the pieces and put them together, I understand something deeply, which makes me feel good

→ **Freedom:** I need to get outside and feel that peace in nature / My work won't take up my evening hours / I want control over my time outside of work and in some ways at work too / I would love a job when I'm outside a lot of the day / When I am outdoors, I feel most free and able to think and focus on my work because my brain is calm

→ **Recognition:** When someone says I did great or I get a good grade, I feel on top of the world / Who doesn't want to feel recognized? / I work really hard, and when a professor recognizes that, I feel like I'm on the right track / When I'm recognized, I feel good and it makes me want to work even harder

→ **Structured work:** no surprises each day / having structure and knowing exactly what I need to do each day for success / I don't like it when something pops up in my day and upends it / I like to know what I need to accomplish and to have the time to accomplish it without surprises / When something blows up my day, it feels chaotic, like I don't have control over my time and schedule

→ **Cultural Learning:** There are people from all over the world at this school, and just hearing how they grew up is fascinating / I like learning how they process information in different ways than I do / if you get outside your comfort zone, you can really learn more about the world just listening to other people talk / Some of my friends are from Thailand, Zimbabwe, France. I've never been to any of those places, but I feel like I have just by listening to their stories / I didn't know how different people grew up and it's fascinating to learn about their identities and how they view the world

→ **Learning:** I love learning something I didn't know before / I like to talk to people who I haven't met before and hear their stories / I like learning about real people and how they act and react to certain situations in their lives / I need to be learning something new each day or I feel like I wasted the day

→ **Authenticity:** Feeling like I can be myself in every situation / feeling understood by my friends and professors / feeling valued by my friends / I want to be me and trust that people will accept me for me with all my great qualities and idiosyncrasies / I want to feel accepted for who I am

→ **Organization:** I am constantly organizing my room, my shelves, my books, my notebooks / I need organization to be able to work and be successful / I like things that have a process to them with a beginning, middle, and end / I'm really good at organizing things and creating processes where there aren't any because I see how things should be / I like knowing where things are and how to move forward / I feel calmer and more at ease when things are organized so I don't have to worry about how to do something or whether something will get done

Sometimes your stream of consciousness will lead you to values that require a *new* stream of consciousness. When that happens, do the same exercise. Once you've written out all your value strings, narrow each one down to the one descriptor or definition that resonates the most. From the above strings, my client's final list looked like this:

→ **Research:** Research is like uncovering different parts of a puzzle . . . when I have all the pieces and put them together, I understand something deeply, which makes me feel good.

→ **Freedom:** When I am outdoors, I feel most free and able to think and focus on my work because my brain is calm.

→ **Recognition:** When I'm recognized, I feel good and it makes me want to work even harder.

→ **Structured work:** I like to know what I need to accomplish and to have the time to accomplish it without surprises.

→ **Cultural learning:** If you get outside your comfort zone, you can really learn more about the world just by listening to other people talk.

→ **Learning:** I like learning about real people and how they act and react to certain situations in their lives.

→ **Authenticity:** I want to feel accepted for who I am.

→ **Organization:** I'm really good at organizing things and creating processes where there aren't any because I see how things should be.

Now it's time to rank your values on a scale of 1 to 5 with 5 being most important. Of course, they are values so they're *all* important, but some will be more important than others.

(5) I can't live without this value being fulfilled.
(4) This value must be fulfilled most of the time.
(3) This value must be fulfilled at least half the time.
(2) It would be nice to fulfill this value some of the time.
(1) This value is not that important if not fulfilled.

Here's an example of how my client's values might be ranked:

→ (5) **Research:** Research is like uncovering different parts of a puzzle . . . when I have all the pieces and put them together, I understand something deeply, which makes me feel good.

→ (5) **Structured work:** I like to know what I need to accomplish and to have the time to accomplish it without surprises.

→ (5) **Authenticity:** I want to feel accepted for who I am.

→ (4) **Organization:** I'm really good at organizing things and creating processes where there aren't any because I see how things should be.

→ (4) **Freedom:** When I am outdoors, I feel most free and able to think and focus on my work because my brain is calm.

→ **(3) Recognition:** When I'm recognized, I feel good and it makes me want to work even harder.

→ **(3) Cultural learning:** If you get outside your comfort zone, you can really learn more about the world just by listening to other people talk.

→ **(2) Learning:** I like learning about real people and how they act and react to certain situations in their lives.

Identifying which values are above 3 is important so you can focus on them when considering a fulfilling job or career. Is it realistic to find a job that meets ALL your values? It is, but you have to invest some extra time to find it. Keep in mind that work values are not the only component when figuring out which job fits you best; you also need to consider *personal values*. Here were some of mine when I was looking for a new job:

→ **Short commute:** No longer than 30 minutes is ideal; more than 40 is a deal-breaker.

→ **Must have daily interaction with others:** Being around people either in person or via video conference.

→ **Meaningful travel:** For real reasons, not just to "make an appearance" somewhere.

→ **No completely open floor plan:** Cubicles and offices are fine but no long tables.

→ **No pets in the office:** No dogs or iguanas (common in the Bay Area!).

→ **Work/life balance:** Flexible arrival/departure (not clocking in or out) and able to attend kids' events (school concerts, sports).

→ **Vacation time:** A minimum of 20 days/year (can start at 15 days + holidays as long as it moves to 20 days within two years) or unlimited paid time off.

You may also have values about the size of the company: Small or big? Which industry? Healthcare, tech, entertainment, financial? Does the company need to be "sexy"? Do you want to read about it in the news? And what about location? Are you willing to move to a new city? If so, are there limits to where? Your list should be much longer than my example above.

By now you're probably thinking, "Yeah, this is a nice dream. Wish me luck finding everything I want. . . ." I never said you'd match every value, but there's no harm in trying!

When Araya graduated from college in Indiana and started interviewing for jobs, she knew she wanted to live in New York. When she was offered a job in advertising at a major tech company, she immediately accepted. "The most thought I put into my decision was that the job would pay the bills and it was in New York." It didn't take long for her to realize there was more to fulfillment than just having any job. "A lot of the aspects about the work were completely misaligned with my true values: independence, creativity, freedom, and learning new things. I didn't have them in the work, and I wasn't given opportunities by my manager to be intellectually stimulated."

Araya knew she had to be more intentional in her next move to find work that aligned with her values. She remembered how much she loved motivational speaking, so she left that job and took some contract work creating social media posts for a few motivational speakers. "I had only been at that job for one-and-a-half years and all my friends had full-time jobs at big companies, so there wasn't a lot of peer support to make the leap from a stable, well-paying job into the freelance world." But she overcame her fear because the contract work aligned with her values. "I don't regret working in corporate because I learned a lot about the basics, from email etiquette to how to understand a client's needs, but I am now much more fulfilled because I am intellectually stimulated, using my creativity every day, and constantly learning. I am in full alignment with my all values!"

Now, she owns her own digital marketing agency and employs one full-time employee and one intern. "I love my job. I know digital marketing is a competitive field, but I provide connection and meaning behind my work and my clients know it's not just a website or a social media post. I am constantly proactively strategizing how to grow their businesses because I care if they are successful." And as Araya's business grows and her life unfolds, she knows her values will also evolve.

Indeed, everyone's values shift and change as they navigate through life. What gives you energy today may be different from what will excite you after the loss of a loved one. What is important to you today may evolve into new or different values when traveling to a new country. But the process of aligning your work to your values will always be the same, for living in alignment with your values is the ultimate source of fulfillment.

Chapter 2 Summary

1. **What do you value?** If you understand your values and live them at work, you will be happy and fulfilled, more engaged and productive. Determine what is important to you at work and in life through a values exercise.

2. **Define your values:** Defining your values isn't hard, but it does take time to zero in on exactly what is important to you and the importance of each value. Creating values strings will help you further hone what your values truly mean for you.

3. **Your values are unique to you:** Be careful to not be virtuous or pick values you think you *should* have or *wish* you had or that your friends have. Your values are unique to you; only you know what is truly important to you.

4. **Rank your values:** Ranking your values from 1 (least important) to 5 (most important) will demonstrate which careers best align with your values and which ones to focus your job search around.

3

What Do You Want to Do?

"The great secret of getting what you want from life is to know what you want and believe you can have it."

—Norman Vincent Peale, minister and author

Every time you seek a new job, from your first one to your last before retirement, you can use your values as the anchor to figure out what you want to do. The number one reason people seek me out as a career coach is because they have no idea what they want to do, in large part because they have not identified their core values.

Recently a woman started telling me about her past jobs in finance and in operations and how she wanted to go into supply chain because she knows she can transfer her skills to that field. I listened patiently and then when she was done, I asked, "I understand you *can* do that, but what do you *want* to do?" She looked at me like I had two heads. Then she said, "I'm not sure I ever thought about what I *wanted* to do." She's not alone.

"What do I want to do?" is a really hard question to answer. If you are scared of making the wrong choice, perhaps nothing sounds interesting to you, or you keep wondering if every choice is "settling" because there might be something better out there. There is one way to settle all this swirl in your head: align your skills with your values to ensure your values will be fulfilled in your career choice.

Tip #3: Align skills with your values to ensure your values will be fulfilled in your career choice.

25

Hard and Soft Skills

First, let's talk skills. All the skills you will use in every job—including your first—are either "hard" or "soft." Hard skills are easier to measure and teach; they include such things as analyzing information, processing payroll, or programming. Certain levels of experience in hard skills are needed for specific jobs. Most of the time, if a person has some hard skills but needs to learn others to be a perfect match for a role, a company will look at their capacity to learn and grow. For example, if someone has learned five kinds of coding programs on their own, some companies may believe they can easily adapt to a new kind of computer programming. If someone has experience analyzing financial data but not human resources data, a company may believe that the person can apply the same analytic skills to a different set of data.

Soft skills, by comparison, aren't used in a specific job; they are needed for *every* job. Soft skills are just as important, if not more important, than hard skills in most jobs.[1] Some examples include "emotional intelligence," "ability to influence," and "interpersonal skills." They define how one is able to act, communicate, and adapt. Soft skills will distinguish higher performers from lower performers and higher productivity from lower productivity. For example, someone with a high level of emotional intelligence will know how to influence through listening rather than speaking. They are self-aware about their own faults and mistakes and react to stressful situations in ways that don't threaten productivity or forward movement. Someone with low emotional intelligence will create a perpetual swirl of conflict, make others around them feel unheard and/or unappreciated, and alienate others from wanting to work for them or even the company. They likely aren't even aware of their negative impact. This type of behavior ultimately leads to lower productivity.

The annual *Future of Jobs Report*[2] from the World Economic Forum shows how soft skills have evolved since 2020. You will notice that some of the top skills needed in the 2023 workforce weren't even considered just three years earlier in 2020.

Top 10 Skills in 2020	Top 10 Skills in 2023
1. Complex Problem-Solving	1. Analytical Thinking
2. Critical Thinking	2. Creative Thinking
3. Creativity	3. Resilience, Flexibility, and Agility
4. People Management	4. Motivation and Self-Awareness
5. Coordinating with Others	5. Curiosity and Lifelong Learning
6. Emotional Intelligence	6. Technological Literacy
7. Judgment and Decision Making	7. Dependability and Attention to Detail
8. Service Orientation	8. Empathy and Active Listening
9. Negotiation	9. Leadership and Social Influence
10. Cognitive Flexibility	10. Quality Control

Interestingly, six of the top ten skills in 2023 are about self-efficacy (#3, #4, #5, and #7) and working with others (#8 and #9). In short, you must master the soft skills of how to "play nice in the sandbox." Complex Problem-Solving was the number one skill valued in the workplace in 2015 and 2020, but in 2023, it is now Analytical Thinking, which is a broader skill. You need analytical thinking to solve complex problems but also to complete technical work and understand how to work with others. Figuring out how analytical thinking aligns with your values should be a top priority.

Other interesting changes over the years include Active Listening, which was in the top 10 in 2015 before it evolved into Emotional Intelligence in 2020. In 2023, Emotional Intelligence was broken down into multiple self-efficacy skills. The book *Emotional Intelligence 2.0* by Travis Bradberry and Jean Greaves[3] identifies the elements of emotional intelligence skills as self-awareness, self-management, social awareness, and relationship management. Look at #3 and #4 in the top skills of 2023: Resilience, Flexibility, and Agility, and Motivation and Self-Awareness. All of these are elements of emotional intelligence.

Cognitive Flexibility in 2020 was about being able to move between assignments and projects and adapt to change and new environments. But today, more is needed. Companies are changing at a rapid pace, merging and consolidating functions and roles. If you have ever worked at a start-up, you get it. As start-ups add people, each person's scope of work narrows, and employees are expected to go deeper into a specific area. Such employees need to enhance their subject matter expertise if they want to support a growing business—and stay employed! The change from Cognitive Flexibility and Emotional Intelligence to Resilience, Flexibility and Agility means not just adapting to change but also recovering quickly from a difficult experience. Not all change will feel good, and, in fact, most of it *won't* feel good, at least initially. Yet employees are still expected to be flexible and agile in changing their mindset no matter how difficult it may be.

I worked at a company that went through three major reorganizations in two years. That's a lot of change. Managers lost their teams. Employees' roles were redefined. One manager was given three different charters and teams of people to manage and lost them just as fast, not because she was a bad manager but because the business was growing so fast that the structure needed to change to keep pace. The key to resilience is whether you can adapt to the change, not just survive it. If you are still complaining months after a shift, you haven't adapted. Also, when work is stressful, what happens to your productivity? If you have resilience, you are able to manage difficult situations mentally through rational thinking and decision making. Further, you are also able to respond to stressful situations and crises by managing your moods, feelings, and emotions. Those capabilities help you adapt to any environmental changes and prevent them from altering your effectiveness.

Further down on the top skills list are the hard skills such as Artificial Intelligence (AI) and Big Data (#15), Programming (#20), Networks and Cybersecurity (#22). Technical skills are important, but if you don't know how to demonstrate leadership skills such as active listening, effective influencing, and proactive communication, it doesn't matter if you are a technical wizard; you won't last long at your company. There's a lot less tolerance these days for the "brilliant jerk." Be sure in your resume to address the top soft skills needed, but also be sure that you know what they mean and are good at them!

Translate Values into Hard and Soft Skills

If you don't know what other skills you have or enjoy using, look back at your values. From those, identify specific hard and soft skills that reflect those values and align with a required skill. Here are a few examples of translating values into hard and soft skills:

Value	Value Definition	Skill
Research	Research is like uncovering different parts of a puzzle . . . when I have all the pieces and put them together, I understand something deeply, which makes me feel good.	**HARD:** research, data analysis, document review, qualitative research methods, quantitative research methods, synthesizing complexity into simplicity, subject matter expertise, experimental design **SOFT:** Critical thinking, curiosity, problem-solving, detail oriented, communication, time management, ethical conduct
Freedom	When I'm outdoors, I feel most free and able to think and focus on my work because my brain is calm.	**HARD:** environmental knowledge, conservation principles, sustainability, environmental and social governance, physical fitness **SOFT:** adaptability, resilience, problem solving, focus, active listening

Value	Value Definition	Skill
Structured work	I like to know what I need to accomplish and to have the time to accomplish it without surprises.	**HARD:** process, structure, goals, design thinking, project management, scheduling **SOFT:** focus, logic, organized, prioritization, formality, independence, trust, work-life balance, communication, attention to detail, problem solving, results oriented
Learning	I like learning about real people and how they act and react to certain situations in their lives.	**HARD:** research, data analysis, psychometric assessments, behavioral understanding, psychology **SOFT:** active listening, critical thinking, effective communication, observation skills, empathy
Organization	I'm really good at organizing things and creating processes where there aren't any because I see how things should be.	**HARD:** process building, business analysis, continuous improvement, Six Sigma **SOFT:** active listening, critical thinking, effective communication, observation skills, empathy

Notice that the list above doesn't mention a specific field. There are numerous fields where these skills would be relevant and the corresponding values fulfilled. In fact, most of the above skills are soft because, as mentioned, they are the skills that will bring you success or failure in any role. They will also be examined the hardest for "culture fit" during the interview process.

If you are struggling with translating your values into hard and soft skills, you can put a prompt into AI programs like ChatGPT or Gemini, such as, "Give me the list of hard and soft skills for Structured Work, which means I like to know what I need to accomplish and to have the time to accomplish it without surprises." While it may not be a complete list, AI can help you get started.

Identify Careers That Fit Your Values

Once you've identified your skills, it's time to start looking at careers that interest you and eliminate those that are clearly wrong. But first, one very important ground rule: while eliminating careers that are clearly wrong, make sure you don't make the critical mistake of eliminating a career based on your lack of experience in that field or the fact that you didn't major in that field or because of concern about pay. We will look at all those considerations later. This exercise is to eliminate careers that you truly know are wrong based on the career itself and/or your interests based on your values. Also, eliminate careers that you don't have an interest in even though they might be obvious choices for your skill set.

For example, I knew I loved to help people, but I couldn't watch a medical show without closing my eyes or looking away during the surgery scenes. Being a nurse or doctor or pursuing any job that involved blood or bodily fluids daily was out. I enjoyed writing and I was good at synthesizing, but I couldn't do math more advanced than the basics, so while research and analysis interested me, any kind of number crunching was out. I loved screenwriting and had completed numerous screenplays, but I couldn't be a screenwriter full-time because one of my top values is stability and that means not having any debt. The screenwriters you hear about who are super successful are the ones who broke through, but most don't, so it would remain a hobby.

Look Outside the Norm for Possibilities

Now that you've eliminated careers that aren't the right fit, it's time to figure out which ones are based on your values and hard and soft skills. This is where the panic sets in for most people. "But I don't know what's out there" is the lament I hear most often. That's right, you don't. But you do have access to unlimited free data on nearly every job that exists including ones you may have never heard of. Where to start? Here:

→ **The Bureau of Labor Statistics** (https://www.bls.gov/ooh/a-z -index.htm) breaks down each occupation group into fastest growing, highest pay, etc. It's a comprehensive list and you may find a career you didn't know existed or never would have thought of that may resonate with you.

→ **World Economic Forum** (www.weforum.org) provides articles on which job sectors are growing and will need workers in future years as well as jobs that may not exist yet but will. Review *The Future of Jobs* reports to find skills needed for all jobs and how in-demand skill sets have been evolving over the years.

→ **Associations.** If you're a whiz at social media and want a job in that field, go to SocialMedia.org and see what kinds of jobs exist and what is required to work in that field. If you're interested in human resources (HR), check out the Society for Human Resource Management (SHRM; https://www.shrm.org/). Associations or groups that focus on one job or field have a plethora of information.

→ **College career sites.** While you are in college, and even if you graduated from college, don't hesitate to explore your college career site. Do you see any posted openings that intrigue you? This is all about research and learning what exists that you may not know about.

→ **Boolean searching on Google.** A Boolean search lists multiple key words for skill areas with modifiers like "and," "or," or "but." Searching key words plus the word "jobs" will also give you an idea of what jobs and careers require your skill set. If I simply Google "coaching, analyzing complex issues, and writing," the search results yield various articles about those subjects, including one about HR and others about executive coaching, writing resumes, or career coaching (go figure!).

You can also try other more generic searches such as . . .

→ **"Best career for someone who enjoys . . . X"** If I replace X with "writing," there are a lot of results. One is a "trade schools" article (https://www.trade-schools.net/articles/jobs-for-writers .asp#jobs-for-writers), which has numerous careers I never would have thought of, including grant writer, content strategist, speechwriter, technical writer, video game writer, social media specialist, web content writer, ghostwriter, and so on.

→ **"Most interesting careers"** for those of you looking for something entirely different nets another trade-schools.net article (https://www.trade-schools.net/articles/unique-careers .asp). A "Professional Bridesmaid"? Who would have thought that such a job existed!

→ **"Best travel jobs"** for those who want to see the world while working delivered an Expert Vagabond article (https://expert-vagabond.com/best-travel-jobs/) and again, there were jobs I didn't even know existed. Then I remembered the three guides from Backroads (www.backroads.com) who led a bike trip I took from Prague to Vienna. One of them had visited more than fifty countries—some for work and some for fun—while traveling on his days off. I remember being instantly jealous that I hadn't thought about doing that in my twenties.

As you look through each job, take your pulse. Are you energized to learn more? Are you just lukewarm when you read the description? You are looking for careers that excite you and make you want to keep researching to learn more. Be careful! Avoid relying on AI to find careers that align with your values. Just as your parents and friends can offer career suggestions, AI can do the same. However, it is essential to explore and discover careers independently, beyond what is merely recommended to you.

I once coached a young woman named Lisa, who had a BA in psychology but never worked in the field. When she graduated from college, she worked as a leasing/marketing coordinator and then a patient/surgical coordinator. They were jobs that paid the bills, but she was bored and had no idea what career to pursue. In our first conversation, she admitted she was lost. I started coaching Lisa and naturally started with helping her define her values. Some of them were . . .

Animals = sense of peace

Shopping = exploring

Designing = my own product that makes me happy

Friends/people = bonding time

Party planning = putting the whole thing together

Being appreciated = I made someone feel good

Exercising outdoors = therapeutic

Working with people = restoring someone's self-confidence

Cleaning = sense of accomplishment

Purpose/passion = happiness and joy for myself and others

Those may seem like a random list as you read them, but the more we talked, three values popped out:

Friends/people = bonding time

Working with people = restoring someone's self-confidence

Passion/purpose = happiness and joy for myself and others

From there Lisa realized that one of her most important values was helping others. Even in her previous roles, she was the one to comfort patients, letting them know that everything would be all right whether it was their medical procedure or their bill. Lisa had pushed away the thought of using her psychology degree because she didn't want to be a traditional psychologist, but she didn't realize she could use it in other roles that were aligned with her values.

She then looked through the Bureau of Labor Statistics list and found numerous roles that interested her and narrowed the list to five possibilities:

→ Child psychologist

→ Organizational psychologist

→ Consumer psychologist

→ Police psychologist

→ Life coach

The only one Lisa knew existed before looking at the BLS list was the first one.

To understand each career a little more, I gave her homework to google all of them individually to learn more about them, including additional schooling or skills needed, and to reflect on what excited her about what she found. She learned, for example, that a child psychologist is a subspecialty of clinical psychology. She would need to get her master's and a PhD and do a one-year internship before completing her PhD. To get licensed, she would need to practice an additional year under supervision. When she took her pulse after reading about it, she reported, "I don't believe I have enough excitement to move forward on this one."

When Lisa researched "organizational psychologist," she learned she would likely need a master's or doctorate degree and that the growth rate for this career is about 35% over the next decade. She learned about its core focus on training and development, compensation and reward systems, and organizational change. Then she remembered that this was the career she had picked when she was getting her bachelor's but had dismissed it at the time because it required a master's degree and she was already overwhelmed just finishing her BA. As Lisa explored it now, years later, she reported remembering why she was so excited about it. "I feel like I would be making a difference in employees' lives and the positions I could get are so varied. I could work for different kinds of companies that focus on things I am passionate about such as animals, design, and fashion."

Once you narrow down your list and find roles that appear interesting, dig in and research the job title using the word "job." For example, I found a job called "chocolate taster." I love chocolate so I googled "chocolate taster jobs" and found an article titled "Cadbury Is Hiring a Chocolate Taster and the Only Qualification Is 'A Passion for Confectionary.'"[4] I mean, wow! It sounded fascinating just by the headline! When I read the story, I learned it was part time. I found another article on *Reader's Digest's* website titled, "5 Secrets about Being a Professional Chocolate Taster,"[5] which was written by Oretta Gianjorio, an actual chocolate taster for Mars Chocolate-UC Davis Chocolate Panel. This valuable research explained the exact nature of the job. It turned out to sound much less glamorous or exciting to me, but others may be enticed to learn more.

Another path to research are actual job descriptions (LinkedIn is a good source). Look at entry-level jobs, then if you find something interesting, look at the same type of job in the same industry but at the level of vice president (VP) or senior vice president (SVP). By looking at the highest job in the field, you can learn all the possible types of work within that career category, and it may broaden your search. You may need to start in that lower level, but this exercise is about learning what the overall career is about, not just pieces of it. The VP or SVP descriptions will show you the trajectory of that career.

Talk to People

Once you have a basic understanding about which career seems interesting and what it will entail, you are ready to ask for "meet and greets" with people who know about or work in that field. Start by reaching out to those you know or someone who knows someone. You have friends. They have friends. Those friends have friends, and all those friends have parents in various fields. And those parents have friends. You get it. You have a wide network of people that probably knows someone in the field you are interested in. Ask one of them to introduce you via email to the person you want to talk with. Once an introduction is made, immediately respond and ask what time works best for them to chat. I am always amazed when someone is interested in a specific career and a colleague of mine agrees to make contact, but the person looking for the meet and greet doesn't follow up. Even if you've changed your mind or remain unsure, respond and/or take the call. You never know what you may learn!

If you don't know someone in your prospective career, I have found that even strangers will give 15 minutes of their time to pick their brains. Just ask Lisa. She reached out to professionals in both life coaching and organizational psychology and learned from coaches themselves that those jobs aren't as stable as she thought. They require constant marketing to find new clients. She realized in talking to them that she had a new value—stability! She wanted to have a reliable job and a title that went with it. That helped her eliminate independent coaching as an option. She used her network and found numerous professionals in organizational psychology to talk to, and every conversation confirmed her belief that this was the right choice. She not only learned about the career itself, she also asked managers what they looked for in hiring so she'd know what practicums and internships to focus on. She reported that each conversation was helpful, and the people were incredibly generous with their time and knowledge.

Of that, I had no doubt. People love to talk about themselves. Lisa did use her network to get introductions to people in the fields she wanted to learn about but also found plenty of strangers to talk with. Without a friend's introduction, reach out to someone you don't know with an email on social media such as LinkedIn, Facebook, and Instagram through their messenger apps. Do some research first and see if you can find a connection (e.g., alumnus of the same college or whether the app shows mutual connections). Without a connection, a simple message can look like this:

Dear [contact name],

Your long career in marketing has given you vast knowledge about the field in every aspect, from the agency side to B2B and B2C companies. I am trying to understand more about marketing and

I'm looking for some advice. I'm hoping you can make yourself available for 15 minutes either on the phone or in person at your convenience to answer some questions about marketing and your own career trajectory in the field. I appreciate your time and hope you can provide your availability to speak

Best,

[your name]

If you have a college connection or you worked with that person in the past, make sure you say that in the first line: "I'm not sure if you remember me, but we worked together at [company name]," or "I'm an alumnus of Georgetown University and I noticed you work in [specific] field." Yes, it's that simple!

Further, if your values have already identified the industry you want to work in (e.g., medical, technology, financial, entertainment), reach out to recruiters in that specific field through LinkedIn. You might be thinking, *Why would a recruiter talk to me?* Not all will. Some won't even respond to your request. But some will if you reach out in a way that is approachable and doesn't beg for a job:

Hi [contact name],

I am looking to land my first job, but I have been having trouble determining where my skills could bring the greatest value to a company. I would love to pick your brain for 15 minutes about how I may be able to position my experience and resume effectively. I have attached my resume for background and hope you can provide your availability to speak.

Best,

[your name]

Again, it's really that simple, but **DO NOT** pitch yourself for a job on these calls, even if you see one that interests you at the company where the recruiter works. You can ask what skills they look for in that type of role but don't sell yourself in any way because that's not the intent of your call. If the conversation goes well, the recruiter may suggest that you reach out if you see anything on the company career site. When you write a thank-you note (and yes, you should write one), that's the time to say you noticed a specific role (if indeed you did) and how you think your skills relate to that role. Meet and greets are designed to learn about a field and build a relationship with the person willing to take your call. If that leads to something more, all the better, but never push it!

I gave this advice to Annie, who was graduating college in six months with numerous marketing internships on her resume but still not convinced she wanted to work in marketing. She emailed and connected to dozens of people over the course of her last year of school targeting different areas of marketing interest (communications, PR, brand, partner, and product marketing). Before she made these calls, she put together a fantastic roadmap for these types of reach-outs and has shared what worked with me. I have also added some suggestions of my own:

→ **Say hello!** Ask casually how his/her day is going and thank the interviewee for taking time to talk to you.

→ **Briefly introduce yourself, why you reached out.** Are you interested in knowing more about the industry/the interviewee's career path? Also, explain how you found him/her. Was it random? Did you have something in common such as graduating from the same college or working at a company where you interned or volunteered?

→ **If the conversation starts flowing organically, stay in the moment without a specific agenda.** Reminder: you are trying to make a "connection" and build a relationship. Some discussions will be a "one and done" and some will lead to long-term mentorship or advice.

→ **Consider asking the interviewee if he/she has any questions *for you* before starting with your own questions.** This step isn't necessary but may be useful if there is any "suspicion" as to why you have so many questions. Just be honest; you are researching the skills needed to be successful in the field and seeking advice for your own trajectory by learning from their success.

→ **Ask questions.** Have a list of potential questions but don't ask them all because it's best to keep the conversation organic and flowing. Examples include:

- What was your journey like from graduating college to where you are now?

- My skills include (fill in the blank), and I'm hoping you can help me understand how to best combine them to bring the greatest value to a company.

- What hard and soft skills do you look for when hiring someone in your field?

- Is there one specific skill that is a "must have" in your field?

- What kinds of decisions do you make on a daily, weekly, or monthly basis?

- What is it about (insert profession) that excites you the most?

- What is the most challenging part of your job?

- What is one thing about this career that people from the outside don't know?

- What skills do you think were necessary to move up in your career?

- If talking to a people manager: What do you look for when hiring someone on your team?

- How have you seen your field change in the time you've been in it?

- I'm trying to wrap my head around "workplace culture." Have you noticed different cultures in the various jobs you've had, and can you describe them?

- In your entire career, is there a company culture you liked the best and why?

- What advice do you have for someone like me trying to break into this field?

- ◆ What is the best piece of advice you received from a former mentor?

- ◆ Is there something you know now that you wish your younger self had known?

After your conversation, don't forget to send a thank-you note via email. A mailed note is fine if you don't have an email address and you know that they go to the office. Someone just took precious time out of their day to give you advice. You are thanking them for their time and expertise. Write that you will keep in touch as you progress in finding your first job, and then do just that. Keep in touch.

Once you've spoken to a person about their career, you've just made a new connection and laid the foundation to build a relationship. Don't lose the connection or torpedo the relationship by disappearing. Also, don't annoy the connection by reaching out every week. There is a rhythm to keeping in touch that is like an art form. I suggest reaching out when something significant happens, such as when you . . .

- → settle on the career of your choice and starting to apply for jobs in the field.

- → finish and pass a certification exam.

- → finish some courses in the field.

- → go back to school to get more experience in a field (shows you are dedicated).

- → have been keeping in touch with your contact for a while and notice they are connected to the hiring manager or someone at the hiring company for a position.

- → are visiting the town your contact is in and you'd love to bring him/her a cup of coffee and visit for 30 minutes. (Be prepared with more questions!)

- → want to wish the contact a happy holiday or a great summer.

- → graduate from college and are on the job hunt.

→ just want to give an update (every six months or so).

→ are on your final interview for a position and would like any final advice.

→ accept a new role. Always circle back with your contacts once you've found a new position so they know where you are and what you are doing.

With the right cadence, a contact may become a mentor or even your boss someday. At the very least, they become a professional relationship. It is therefore important to maintain communication but not become a burden or a pest: "Hey, just thought I'd check to see if you are you working on anything interesting?" Remember, this is a professional contact, not a friend. They may be kind and generous with their time, but they aren't sharing their daily lives with you. It's like having a coach. Coaches don't mingle their own lives with those of their clients. The focus is on the client. The same goes for the person who is looking for their first job. The focus is on you and that is okay!

So when you reach out to a contact, it should only be about asking for advice, providing an update, or, if you've built a longer-standing relationship over time, you can ask for your colleague to refer you to a company that has a role you found. Notice I said "a role you found." My favorite example of the wrong way to stay in touch is when someone sends a contact their updated resume and asks if they've "heard of any jobs" out there. Most people aren't in the job market or in the job market at your level. By asking contacts to let you know if they've "heard about any openings," you are implying that they do your job search for you. Once you've built a solid relationship and your contact believes you could be a solid contributor to a team, he/she will automatically keep you in mind if they hear about an opportunity that is right for you.

If there is a position at your contact's company and you've built a rapport, ask if they have any information on the role beyond the job description or whether the role reports to your contact. If they feel comfortable with you, he/she may offer to refer you for the role without you even asking. If it's at another company, ask your contact if they know anything about that other company—the leadership, the culture, and/or the role itself.

Stop!

Okay, now stop. Take your pulse (not literally, figuratively). How are you feeling? Are you overwhelmed with what it takes to find your first job? Don't fear! My client Lisa felt overwhelmed at first and described herself as feeling "down" and "hopeless" because she didn't know how to go forward. But once she started talking to people, I could hear the excitement in her emails and voice when we spoke about what she was learning. When I asked her if she was still feeling confident that this was the right path, her answer was clear. "At first I thought I'd have to take a crappy job and hope to work myself up. Now I know what I want to do and I'm super excited for the future. This process has opened up a whole new world for me. . . . I feel really good and energized." That is the feeling you are looking for—excitement about your future.

Don't Give Up

It may take dozens of phone calls in a single field to learn it's not the right one for you, but it can only take one call to set your trajectory. When I was looking for a new career, I had no idea what I wanted to do, and I wasn't sure if my skills were transferable to any new career. In fact, I could count on one hand the number of people in the entire country who did exactly what I did. It was like starting all over after graduating college.

I did the steps above and I narrowed down my choices to public relations or some type of communications like corporate communications or internal communications because I loved writing and formulating messages and giving advice on how to position an issue. My second thought was to work as a legislative assistant—someone who drafts and edits state or federal legislation, including bills or rules, and who helps propose and research ideas for legislation. I know that's an odd combination, but I majored in political communication in college and part of my most recent position dealt with immigration: moving production crews around the world and bringing in talent for shows like the *MTV Movie Awards* and Nickelodeon's *Kids' Choice Awards*. In fact, I became so interested in immigration that by the time I left, I was giving advice internally without outside counsel help. I also worked with our internal lobbyists to get language in the "Gang of 8" immigration bill (known as the Border Security, Economic Opportunity, and Immigration Modernization Act of 2013), which allowed reality show participants to perform on unscripted television (e.g., *The Real Housewives*) on a visitor's visa when not part of a competition show. I loved working on that project even though the bill never made it to law.

So, I started reaching out to people in those fields. As expected, some people didn't return my email or LinkedIn messages. Some said they were too busy to talk to me. After a woman on LinkedIn accepted my request to connect, I emailed her a nice invitation to speak for 15 minutes about what she does as a legislative aid. She wrote back immediately. "I knew if I connected to you it would be a risk that you would want something and I'm running for a city council seat right now and don't have time to talk." I thought, hmmm, I won't be voting for you! Eventually, at least one person in both the public relations/communications and legislative assistant fields agreed to talk to me. Unfortunately, both conversations left me more lost than ever and feeling that neither career was a perfect fit. The PR-type roles seemed boring. I couldn't imagine writing press releases or hounding the press all day for coverage and determining my success based on how many "impressions" each story received. The legislative assistant role was overwrought with politics. Surprise! I knew I'd get frustrated if something never moved forward. I would also have had to move to Sacramento (the capital of California) or DC.

I decided to reach out to recruiters. On LinkedIn, I happened upon one recruiter from eBay at the time, who wrote on his profile, "If you need career advice, happy to give it!" Great, I thought, and I wrote him a simple LinkedIn message:

Hi Nathan,

I saw on your LinkedIn Profile that you would be willing to give career advice. I am looking to transition to a new career, but I have been having trouble determining where my skills could be most effective in a company. I would love to hear your perspective about how I may be able to transfer my skills. I know your time is valuable and would only need about 15 minutes.

Best,
Marlo

Note that I mentioned how my skills could be most effective *to a company*. I learned early in my career that it's not all about me. When looking for a new job, it's about finding a hole that needs to be filled *and* filling it with your skills. Most people are looking through the lens of "What do I want to do?" That's a great place to start, but you will have to translate how your skills are transferable and will directly benefit that company. In writing the message the way I did, I wanted to make sure the recruiter knew I was looking for the right fit, not just any new job. He was nice enough to write back and we scheduled a call at his first available time, six weeks later. Little did I know this would be the single most important and informative call I had initiated and the catalyst for my career transition.

I started the conversation by thanking him for his time; I knew it was valuable and he didn't have to take a call from a random stranger. I explained that I thought he might be able to help me since he'd been a recruiter at numerous companies in various fields. I didn't assume he had looked at my LinkedIn profile, so I explained that the reason I reached out was because I had these unique and diverse skills, had explored a number of fields such as PR/communications and government affairs, and knew they weren't for me. I explained my broad background (lawyer mind, analytical skills, immigration and risk expertise, TV reporting, and communication skills) and that I didn't know what to do with it all.

He asked me a few questions about what I loved about my current job. I had my values list in front of me and explained that I really enjoyed coaching, mentoring, advising, solving problems, and working cross- functionally. I loved being a part of a company that felt relevant to my life.

He said, "It sounds like you may like being an HR business partner." I politely explained that I'd thought of HR but wasn't interested in doing typical HR work, like harassment trainings and investigations or processing leaves of absence. He said, "No, the job's not tactical, like helping people file for leaves of absence. It's strategic, working alongside leadership to help the business grow through talent and determining what people skills are needed to do that." He also explained that the job involves working with senior executives on organizational effectiveness and organizational design. Huh, I thought. I had only known HR people to be generalists. I had never met a strategic HR person in my nearly twenty years of working and in fact had no direct interaction with HR in any of my previous jobs. Clearly, my perception was not the reality. He suggested doing some research and look only for HR business partner positions that had the word "coaching" in the job description. I thanked him for his time and promptly started researching.

It didn't take long to realize that there are many jobs titled "HR business partner" and none of them are the same. Some were tactical as I'd assumed: administering benefits and compensation. Some were focused on creating learning and development programs. Some were more operations based. And some were very strategic, as Nathan had explained. I never realized that one job could have so many variations. I looked at each description, the size of the company, the industry the company was in, and so on. I couldn't find a pattern because each company viewed the HR business partner job differently, though I did find the strategic HR business partner roles mostly in tech companies.

He was also right that the jobs I most resonated with had the word "coach" in them. I called a colleague who had left Viacom not long before and was now the chief people officer at a start-up tech company. She filled me in about how the HR business partner role works inside companies.

I also mentioned my information quest to a friend who told me that a former sorority sister of ours was a successful executive business coach and could be a great lead. I called her and she explained that coaching is not mentoring, or advising like a consultant, but a more formal way of helping someone realize their potential. So far, everything sounded great. Now I just needed to figure out how to show that my skills were transferable.

Repeat this chapter over and over until you have landed on a potential career (or two) that you want to pursue. You may decide on one, but as you learn more about it, you may discover that it sounded much better than it is in real practice. Being a lawyer is a great example. Some people love practicing law, but many realize in their first law job, it's not what they thought. Being a lawyer is mostly about writing, positioning, influencing, interpreting, and negotiating. That means sitting behind a desk and reading and writing most of the day. Unless a lawyer pursues civil litigation or criminal law as a practice area, they may never perform in front of a jury. Most attorneys push paper; their jobs are not the exciting dramas you see on TV.

Alternatively, you may hear about a career that sounds boring until you dig in and learn the nuances. I always thought HR was about processing leaves of absence and hiring and firing people. I had no idea how much fun it could be working behind the scenes, influencing senior leaders to be better leaders, communicators, and managers, and helping employees adapt to change. So, be like a detective trying to uncover clues—the good as well as the bad—to help you solve the case of the elusive dream career.

Chapter 3 Summary

1. **Hard and soft skills:** Align your values to hard and soft skills used in the workplace.

2. **Determine "no" careers:** Figure out which careers would use your values-aligned hard and soft skills but you absolutely can't

do even though they seem like obvious choices based on your college major or interests.

3. **Find potential careers:** Look at the BLS website and other websites that list career positions in every field. Narrow down choices that excite you.

4. **Research careers:** Research all possible careers and look at job descriptions to further narrow down choices.

5. **Talk to people:** Set up phone or in-person "meet and greets" to gain more insight into careers you may not know about and then build relationships with people in those fields.

6. **Repeat:** If you did all the steps in this chapter and still have not landed on a career that excites you, do it again. You may have shortchanged yourself in one of the steps or missed a career that is perfect for you.

Experience Comes in Many Forms

"An investment in knowledge pays the best interest."

—Benjamin Franklin, a founding father of the United States

Now that you've narrowed down your potential career choices, it's time to get real. Do you need additional education? Do you need specific skills like multilanguage fluency? Do you need a certification? Even if you don't need anything else to do the job you've chosen, how do you show potential employers you are serious about landing a job in your chosen career?

Determine Needed Job Skills and Experience

Tip #4: Research the types of degrees, certifications, languages, and/or experience you will need or should have for your chosen career.

Many jobs don't require a higher degree, such as in law or practicing medicine. Where no advanced education is required, it is up to you to determine what additional undergraduate courses, internships, volunteer activities, or certifications you may need. The four easiest places to find answers are LinkedIn profiles, job descriptions, meet and greets, and Google/AI programs.

1. LinkedIn profiles: These are great sources of information for both introductions and learning about different career paths. Look for patterns. Does everyone have an MBA or a higher degree or a bachelor's in a specific major? If you want to work in an international job, what kind of fluency shows up in these profiles? When looking at experience, do you see the use of data? And if so, which data sets are most prominent in a particular field? Do you see specific kinds of projects? Repetitive words? LinkedIn profiles are great for figuring out the true crux of a specific job and the types of skills, degree, or certification needed to be successful.

2. Job descriptions: Job descriptions are also full of information. Research VP and SVP roles as well as entry-level positions in your chosen career to identify patterns of experience and formal education. Look at job requirements, desired qualifications, and language skills needed. "Required" technically means "necessary," but you'd be surprised at how many requirements aren't really required. For example, there was a "required 30% travel" for my HR job. I traveled twice in the first year. So, don't dismiss a job just because there's a requirement you don't have or one that makes you feel uneasy unless it's an obvious reach, such as working in France with fluency in French.

"Desired" or "preferred" qualifications means a recruiter is looking for someone with a certain degree or level of experience and will give such resumes a closer look, but it's not a deal breaker if you don't have them.

For a general sense of what the role requires, look for repetitive words or job duties. For example, in the strategic HR roles I sought out, I saw "coach" on multiple lines. I had coached my previous direct reports and some cross-functional colleagues, but I thought there may be more to this "coaching" thing, so I started researching "executive coach" and "certification." I learned that there were lots of certification courses, but I couldn't figure out if I definitely needed to take them and, if so, which ones. So . . .

3. Meet and greets: Asking the right questions in meet and greets about necessary education or certifications will also help you determine if you have—or can get—all the requirements. During my transition, I again called on some of my previous contacts and talked to new ones as well. In general, they didn't think getting certified in coaching was absolutely necessary, but we also agreed that it would be hard to show I had coaching experience based on my current role. That meant getting certified.

Lisa learned when talking to people in industrial/organizational psychology that she only needed a bachelor's degree. But she viewed getting her master's degree and using those school years to secure a bevy of internships and a practicum as ways to gain relevant experience she didn't already have on her resume from undergrad internships.

4. Google/AI: Try different combinations such as "career name + credential" or "education + position" or "career name + certification." You can also ask ChatGPT or Gemini, "What degree, certifications, or other knowledge is required to be a physician's assistant and what schools or companies offer those programs?" Most careers don't need an advanced degree or a specific credential but do have certification programs. For example, HR has different certifications including PHR (Professional Human Resources), SPHR (Senior Professional Human Resources), and GPHR (Global Professional Human Resources). The Society for Human Resource Management (SHRM) also has comparable certifications such as the SHRM-CP (Certified Professional) and SHRM-SCP (Senior Certified Professional). While they may be "desired" or "preferred," none of them are *required* to work in HR. And neither company's certifications are more prestigious than the other. Also, colleges and universities offer master's programs as well as certificates in human resources but these, too, are not required to work in the field. So why bother?

The biggest benefit of working toward a certification or an advanced degree in your area of interest is that you can learn about the field both tactically and philosophically. You may also end up doing projects while earning a degree or certification, which can be used on your resume as experience. Finally, once you have some knowledge about a field or a specific position, you will have more to talk about during meet and greets and potential interviews. For example, if someone in HR asks you, "Can you give me an example of a time you had to help an employee with a problem?" you will probably have a good answer!

Another Google/AI search could focus on skills such as "Skills needed to be a great data analyst." A plethora of results will pop up, but some basic skills are Microsoft Excel, SQL, R or Python, data visualization, and machine learning. A few soft skills might include presentation skills, critical thinking, and distilling large amounts of information into actionable insights. By knowing what skills are needed, you can determine what courses are available to learn them and whether you can gain practical experience in those skills in your internships, volunteer opportunities, or in a job.

Finally, if you google or AI search for "What are the most in demand professional certifications," you'll find on Google an *Entrepreneur* article listing the top nine certifications. Topping the list is the CAPM (Certified Associate in Project Management) from www.pmi.org.[1] You will find similar results of Project Management Professional (PMP) on ChatGPT.com. Why is it ranked number one? Because project management skills are essential for entry-level positions across all fields, as well as throughout your entire career. Obtaining this certification will provide you with foundational knowledge that can distinguish you from other entry-level applicants with minimal work experience.

How many of these skills and how much experience do you need for your very first job? As many and as much as possible. You want to show your drive to work in your chosen career through the steps you've taken to get there: researching the field, talking to people, making time to obtain a degree or certification, and taking internships or volunteer opportunities. Sometimes dedication and drive are the only distinguishing factors between you and another candidate. Of course, the pursuit of additional courses, certifications, or higher degrees will require some resources.

Develop Skills and Experience

Once you know what experience and skills you need, look for inexpensive ways to gain the necessary knowledge.

1. Free courses: If you want to go back to school, look for colleges that offer reduced or even free tuition. For example, want to become a software engineer and only pay tuition if you get a job? Check out institutions such as the Holberton School (https://www.holbertonschool .com) and Make School (https://www.makeschool.com/). Other options include your local community college or local university "extension" classes for those not enrolled as full-time students. UCLA (https://www .uclaextension.edu/) has hundreds of such courses and some are online. *U.S. News & World Report* found that some schools will offer free tuition if you give back afterwards or come from certain states or socioeconomic backgrounds.[2] Alice Lloyd College, for example, offers free-tuition education for full-time students from the counties that surround the Central Appalachian service area. Some schools offer free tuition in exchange for working on campus.

If a full-time commitment isn't an option, or you just want to take a few courses or get a certificate in a specific area, consider Coursera (www .coursera.com), which is a hot site for free courses. A Forbes article touts Udemy.com, an online resource for courses created by content creators in fifty languages.[3] Codecademy.com is free and will teach you how to code in different programming languages for careers in data science, web programming, and software engineering. Stanford Online also offers free courses and certificates in numerous areas including project management, predictive modeling, clean energy, mathematics, and engineering. Finally, consider investing in a membership to LinkedIn Learning (www.linkedin learning.com/learning). There you can learn how to master both hard skills from Excel to SQL and soft skills from "Preparing for Successful Communication" to "Managing Office Politics."

2. Internships, volunteering, freelancing: Despite having certifications and/or a degree in your field of interest, many entry-level positions still require one-to-three years' experience. That may seem unfair, but there are strategies to position yourself as someone who *has* the relevant experience.

Internships: If you are still in school and/or can show internship eligibility, you can register at a local college for available opportunities. This is the easiest way to gain the experience and skills needed for your chosen field.

Belle M. majored in music communications at Northeastern University, but she needed an internship to hone in on exactly what she wanted to do in the industry.

Her first internship was in artist management. "You deal with every aspect of an artist's career," she explained, "and while I liked it for a year, it would have been a lot to handle as a long-term commitment. But I learned I liked the digital marketing part of it." So, she targeted her next internship to gain experience in digital. "At Sony Music, I focused on four things that were very executional, including creating media plans, launching ads, reporting on the ads performance, and communicating with different partners and labels. I really enjoyed it, but I missed working on frontline projects." For her third internship, she secured a frontline digital marketing internship with RCA Records. "I worked on social media plans to connect artists with fans. I am getting closer and closer to what I want to do because I now know that I definitely want to work directly with fans and artists."

Belle has gained all the skills and experience she needs for an entry level job in the music industry. "I journal every day and log everything I do whether it's a big team project, a small task, or a coffee chat. I write down what I learned, what skills I used, and how I brought value, so I'll able to discuss that when I am interviewing for my first job." Brilliant idea!

Volunteering: If you are unable to secure an internship, consider volunteering for a family member or acquaintance, your place of worship, a community center, or local charities in your field of interest. Generally, you won't be asked whether you were paid for your work; simply provide the months and year(s) of your involvement on your resume.

Freelancing: If you are entrepreneurial minded, establish an LLC or register as a sole proprietorship in your state and join platforms such as Upwork, Toptal, and Fiverr to take on freelance projects. These experiences will not only build your confidence and credibility but also allow you to showcase relevant projects on your resume under the name of your company. Plus, you may gain valuable references along the way or realize that you can support yourself freelancing and enjoy the flexibility!

3. Accepting a "less-than-perfect" job opportunity: This may seem counterintuitive when this entire book is about finding a job in a fulfilling career. But sometimes you need a first job to gain some experience and build relationships, which you can leverage toward the "perfect job." There is nothing wrong with accepting your first job simply to gain skills that you will use in future jobs.

My niece, Tali, is a perfect example. She graduated with numerous marketing internships on her resume and interviewed at several companies to work in sports marketing—her chosen career. "I gave it my best shot. I spent every day for five months looking for a job, and I did get some interviews through my network." But in a competitive market, she was unable to secure a position in sports marketing without "real" work experience outside of internships, so she chose to accept her first post-college job as a sports and entertainment media *planner* at a fast-growing media services agency. "I call this job 'sports marketing adjacent.' While it isn't my dream sports marketing job, it is helping me build foundational work skills every college graduate needs. I am learning the entire process of activating a marketing campaign, the technology used, and the people you need to align with in the process." She says she still has contact with the sports world supporting a major streaming service in its advertising goals and is very happy with her decision. "Something that was preached to me and I hold onto is that getting your foot in the door in the industry you want to be in is key. Nothing is perfect, and if you get hung up on perfection for your first job, you won't find one or gain any useful experience. I know the skills that I'm adding to my resume will jump out to future sports marketing companies."

What Tali learned early in her career is that every opportunity is about learning and growing and being open minded about whatever is in front of her. She continuously aligns her work with her values, and says this job is providing as much value to her in building skills as she is bringing to the job.

Time

As you learn what additional education or experience you may need to launch into your chosen career, you will want to determine a realistic timeline for finding that first job. Set expectations for yourself so you don't get frustrated about how long it may take to set yourself up for success. Perhaps you need to take a lower-paying job or that less-than-perfect job not in your chosen field. Maybe your parents can support you a bit longer with a mutually agreed deadline. I can't wave a magic wand and tell you how long it will take to land your first professional job because there are just too many variables, including your experience, how you interview, the network you've built and how you leverage it, where you want to live and whether you are willing to move, whether you are willing to work onsite versus remote. . . . The list goes on.

Employer Support

If you happen to be working your way through college or graduate school and are considered an exceptional employee, you may be able to transition to a job in your chosen career within your current company. Most employers don't want to lose an employee they value, even if your interest lies in a different department at the company. Find out if your company has people who work in your chosen career. Most companies have marketing, human resources, legal, finance, and business development departments. Ask for a "stretch assignment" from a colleague in the department you want to work in to gain skills, build relationships, and prove your capabilities.

One of my former employees on the production risk team at Viacom was getting an MBA with a specialty in data science. While part of our job was to analyze background checks, psych exams, and medical exams to determine the level of risk for reality-show candidates, it didn't rise to the level of data science. To support her degree work, I gave her as many analytic projects as I could so she could gain some practical experience, but I could tell she was frustrated, and her work was starting to falter.

After a few months of watching her go through the motions of her job but clearly lacking passion for it, I sat her down and asked her softly, "What's going on?" She admitted that she just wanted to be like everyone else in her class—interning and learning from brilliant data scientists— but she couldn't leave her day job because she supported her family. She felt stuck. She finally knew what she wanted to do but thought this degree would be a waste of time without practical experience. I listened and asked her what her ideal job would be when she graduated. She said working as a data scientist in a media company. I mentioned she probably missed the deadline to interview for paid summer internships, so I said I would help her get one at our company. I offered to call the head of our data science team (whom I didn't know) to see if they'd be interested in interviewing my employee for an internship. They had already hired all the interns they had budgeted to hire for the summer, so I made it easy by saying I'd make her available full-time for six weeks while drawing a salary from my budget, not theirs. She interviewed and they offered her a summer internship.

On the day she left, I walked into her office and declared my intention with these exact words: "Don't come back." I told her there were numerous openings in that department (listed on the company's jobs page) and my expectation was that she would fight for one of those roles by completing a stellar internship. She thanked me and I didn't hear another word.

About halfway through her internship, two managers in the data science department offered her their open positions. After much debate, she accepted one of them and honed her skills. Find your champion— someone who will help you get the experience you need to move to a role that fulfills your values. If you find that support from your manager, make sure you keep excelling in your current role.

Unfortunately, not every manager or company will be willing or is able to give an employee the same kind of opportunity. Even though my boss knew I was working on my certification in executive coaching and that

I wanted to learn more about organizational design, I got little support. My manager was adamant in telling me, "People spend their entire careers in those areas. There will no opportunity for you to learn them in your present role." So, I coached at night and on weekends and found HR leaders outside my company who described how they approached organizational design and organizational talent planning.

If you can't find opportunities at your current employer to gain some of the skills needed for a new career, consider volunteering at night or on weekends with a nonprofit or your religious place of worship. Ask a friend in the field if you can shadow one of their projects or meet to discuss steps on something they are working on. Just don't let your outside activities affect your current work or school performance.

Once you've gained the knowledge and experience to move into your chosen career, and you want to do it at your current company, your boss won't support you if you aren't already an exceptional employee. "Showing up well" means having a good attitude, doing your job, and going above and beyond in your current role. If you let your work slack because you plan to leave in a few months, your boss may not support your candidacy in another department. So even if you've mentally moved on from your current college job, show up well every day and perform at your best. Use every opportunity to learn and grow, especially in soft skills because those are universal and needed for success in every job.

After being told there was no way to advance my skills in my current role or in a different role at my company, I continued to perform at an exceptional level and took the time to set myself up for success. That meant three months of studying at night and on weekends to prepare for the SPHR and GPHR certification exams and nearly a year to get certified in executive coaching. A year! I also took all my continuing legal education classes to keep my law license after I changed careers in case it didn't work out and so I wouldn't be worried. I took online courses on soft skills through my company's learning portal and read a few books such as *The Start-Up of You*[4] by Reid Hoffman and Ben Casnocha and *The First 90 Days*[5] by Michael Watkins to jazz me up about a new role.

You don't need to be an overachiever. Take your time to gain the core skills, knowledge, and education you need to secure your first job. The more certifications, degrees, classes, and experience you can show, the more likely you'll convince a hiring manager that you are working to truly understand the substance of a field and how it is practiced in the workplace. Patience is critical when you are investing in you.

Chapter 4 Summary

1. **Determine needed skills and experience:** Research degrees, certifications, and experience needed for your chosen career through reviewing LinkedIn profiles and job descriptions, taking meet and greets, and googling positions and skills.

2. **Develop skills and experience:** Determine how to gain skills and experience through taking additional courses, internships, volunteering, or freelancing and what it will cost.

3. **Determine time frame:** Based on your needs and situation, identify a realistic time frame to gain additional degrees, certifications, skills, and experience.

4. **Find supporters:** If working or interning within six months of graduation, look within your current company or outside your company to find supporters and mentors who will help you gain relevant experience.

CHAPTER

5

Learning the Lingo
to Transfer Skills

"Learning a new language is becoming a member of the club—
the community of speakers of that language."

—Frank Smith, contemporary psycholinguist

As we've been discussing, if you dream of working in a specific career, you will need to figure out how to truly understand the field you've chosen and how your skills are directly applicable. The problem is that . . . you can't. Networking and job descriptions can help, but it's like reading a book on how to make a pizza versus doing it. Moving into your very first career is similar. Since you haven't lived it yet, you will need to learn as much as you can about it and speak in ways that show you've done your homework and are serious about the career.

Tip #5: Learn the lingo to understand your chosen field and hone your message.

Learning the Lingo through Conversations

In 2016, LeEco was a tech darling. The company had just taken over a large campus in San Jose and was in the news daily for its offer to acquire Vizio. I connected with the VP of people operations on LinkedIn and he was willing to meet with me. We talked for quite a while as he explained the difference between what he did compared to the HR business partner roles I was considering. This helped me further understand the nature and structure of human resources. He told me about the roles he had open on the operational side and thought it would be easier for me to transfer into one of those based on my experience. He was probably right, but as he described them, I knew they weren't right for me because I wanted to be business-facing and more strategic in my work with people. He also told me that operations roles aren't a natural gateway to HR business partner. By the end of our conversation, he offered to let me use his name to connect with the VP of HR business partners at LeEco. I emailed the VP and he agreed to a phone call.

This was a critical meeting. I was almost finished with my coaching courses and had just passed the HR certification exams. I had been researching and doing meets and greets for months and learning as much as I could about working in HR. I was ready to start applying for jobs. But since this was an informational meet and greet meeting only, I couldn't pitch myself directly for the open HR business partner roles at LeEco. My goal was to subtly convince him I was worthy of an in-person interview. While sitting in the parking lot of my final coaching class waiting for his call, I was thinking about how much I loved the coaching courses and helping people challenge themselves to overcome obstacles to be the best version of themselves. Finally, my phone rang. I answered, "Hi, this is Marlo." Then I blew it.

After the usual pleasantries, the first question he asked me was, "Why do you want to be an HR business partner?" I answered, "I want to help people." It was top of mind as I was about to enter my last coaching course in thirty minutes. He immediately said, "Wrong answer." He went on to explain that the main goal of HR business partners is to align people's skills with the goals of the business. Of course, I knew that from studying for my certifications and from previous conversations on organizational design, but I hadn't been using that as the crux of my message.

I knew in that moment I had lost any chance to interview in person for an HR business partner role at LeEco (even though it was a blessing; a week later, the China-based company started pulling out of San Jose). What felt like one of the worst meet and greets I ever had turned out to be one of the most helpful in teaching me how to use the right lingo to position myself for the role I wanted. From that day forward, I answered that same question more than a dozen times in language that was understood by HR leaders.

Connecting Skills

Once you understand the field you've chosen and the lingo used, it will be easier to connect how your skills from previous jobs, internships, school leadership positions and volunteer activities are directly applicable to those needed for the job. When I wanted to transition into HR, I had more than a decade of TV news reporting experience and more than a decade of business risk experience. Just like you may have internships or volunteer experience, but perhaps no real work experience when graduating college, I had no actual experience *in* HR. Notice, I said "*in* HR." I did have HR experience. Both of my previous jobs focused on people in different ways. The words underlined below connect my TV news experience with the world of HR.

My news jobs required me to *influence* people to talk with me on camera or provide information under difficult circumstances, such as after a loved one had passed away and I knocked on the door of a family who had just lost a child or a husband or a mother. I had less than three seconds to convince people to talk to me, hopefully on camera, or that door would slam in my face. That means I also had to be <u>authentic</u>. Because the news aired every night at set times, I was always working in a <u>fast-paced environment</u> with a hard deadline. If I wasn't successful, there would be a "hole" in the newscast. As an investigative reporter, I had to <u>research and source the truth</u> and <u>distill a lot of information</u> into a simplified story that could be understood. Finally, I had to have <u>on-air presence</u> when presenting stories to the public.

On the surface, it doesn't appear that my TV news work had anything to do with HR, but if you look at the skills needed in HR, there was plenty of relevance. For example, it's critical to <u>source the truth during an in-house investigation</u> to discover the root of a problem when two departments or two people aren't getting along and jeopardizing <u>company productivity</u>. Presenting live and on air provided me with <u>executive presence</u> and <u>presentation skills</u>, which I continue to use today, especially in front of the C-suite (the most senior people at the company, e.g., CEO: chief executive officer; COO: chief operating officer; CMO: chief marketing officer, etc.). Finally, many companies think they are fast-paced, but nothing is faster than turning around a story every day for the 5 p.m. news when your photographer isn't available until 3 p.m., or breaking news happens at 4:30 p.m. and you need to go live with it in 30 minutes. HR requires someone who <u>can maintain executive presence under pressure, deal with uncomfortable conversations, influence in an authentic way</u>, and work at an <u>incredibly fast pace</u>. See how it all connects when you look at your previous work and role through the lens of the new role?

Working in "production risk" also focused on people—reality-show participants. Every reality show needs certain people who "<u>fit</u>" in the overall cast to make it successful and <u>drive business</u> (aka viewership). Have you ever noticed that most shows have one person who can be edited to look "crazy"? Or the "smooth talker," the "maternal mom"? In reading thousands of reality participant psychological reports and background checks and then watching those personalities play out on set, I <u>understood all kinds of people on a deeper level</u>. I also had to evaluate how I thought each person would <u>perform under the pressure</u> of glaring lights and television cameras and whether they could cope after production and when the show aired. When the show went into production, I would deal with <u>crisis management</u> when people clashed in an unacceptable or dangerous way on set. At times, some of them regretted what they had said on camera and would threaten to harm themselves if a show aired. I had to intervene during or after production to ensure they and the rest of the cast and crew were safe, while <u>coaching TV producers and company executives</u> on what to do. Pull the show? Keep airing it? I had to use <u>exceptional judgment</u> to constantly <u>manage sensitive situations</u> while keeping productions moving forward, because if the production shut down or the network pulled the show, that could mean a loss of millions of dollars.

I have other examples from other positions and experiences, but you get the picture. With all those skills, it wasn't hard to connect them to HR business partner skills. HR recruiting is about hiring people who have the right fit for the role both from a skills perspective and a culture perspective. My management experience combined with my unique ability to understand people on a deeper level—how to look at their skill sets and where they could stretch their skills—would allow me to help align those skills with business goals. Also, I had an ability to coach senior executives on what would positively (or negatively) impact their business. A stretch? Sure, but still a connection of skills.

Using HR terminology to describe the work I did as a business leader outside of HR showed I was "doing" HR without actually "being" in HR. By connecting the two skill sets and learning the lingo, I was able to open doors. And that's the key; learning the right language will align any previous experience to your dream career and convince a hiring manager to see how you would bring a unique perspective to the role.

Bringing a Unique Perspective

Without insulting people who spent their entire career in HR, coming from outside HR gave me unique insights into the people, pressures, and priorities of a business. Experience gained from previous or current work, internships, and volunteer activities, no matter how different the work was compared to the new career, will give you a fresh perspective on the new career. Please repeat this because it's so important: your experience from previous internships, jobs, and volunteer experiences will give you a fresh perspective on the new career. Taking that perspective and using the lingo of the new career to describe your current experience will show a hiring manager that you'll bring something to the position that no other candidate has. That will be appealing to growth-minded hiring managers because most of them have been in their roles for a long time and are seeking fresh perspectives.

Ben is a perfect example of someone who had a career that seemingly wasn't applicable to any other. He was working on film and television sets in "physical asset management," in charge of all the props and making sure the sets were dressed (decorated) for each day's shoot. He was working crazy hours and wanted nothing more than to find a career that had more work–life balance and would have career growth. Once his assignment on a TV show or film finished, he had to fight for the next job, never knowing how long he'd be unemployed before landing the next gig. But set dressing? How is that applicable to any other career outside of film and TV production? He had some experience as an executive assistant to film producers and literary agents and some other project management experience, but there was no common thread through his decade of work experience.

At first, he explored moving into production safety because he understood safety from a set dressing perspective and knew it was a field that lacked enough people for all the work. He knew some of the Occupational Safety and Health Administration (OSHA) requirements from being on sets and working with the safety directors, and had picked up enough lingo to keep an interview going. To shore up his knowledge, he completed some OSHA certification courses he knew he would need and would also help him with additional lingo. Then he honed his message and unique perspective that his years on sets made him a better candidate than someone with just OSHA knowledge, because he understood that set dynamics and his various roles and responsibilities would make it easy for him to influence a crew to comply with safety requirements.

As he started to interview for production safety roles at some of the largest studios, confident he could translate his current work to the new role and fulfill some of his values—such as having a stable paycheck and being more independent—he knew that becoming a production safety executive wouldn't fulfill his most important value. He would still be working crazy hours and for weeks at a time, often traveling around the world, which would keep him away from his family. The closer he got to this new career, the more he realized the sacrifice he'd be making—a sacrifice that almost seemed worth it just to get out of the set dressing world, which was becoming intolerable.

As he was in the final rounds of interviews at a major studio for a production safety job, I heard about a role in content operations at Roku.

I was told the technical aspects of the job could be learned and that the hiring manager needed someone who understood processes and people and had a great attitude. The role was hard to fill because most people didn't want to leave full-time employment for a full-time freelance job, which Ben was already doing. There was also very little on his resume that would scream he had the right skills or that he'd even be interested, but I mentioned the role to him anyway and he jumped at the opportunity. I was clear that while I could get him a screening interview, I could not get him the job. He had to do that by convincing the hiring manager he was a fit for the role, so I encouraged him to start by learning the lingo and finding a common thread in his current and former jobs to create a "unique perspective."

He went after it with vigor and quickly educated himself on the lingo of that type of work and the technology used, such as "title tracking," "file ingestion," "content delivery," "metadata," "technological systems," and "workflows." He couldn't actually say he worked with metadata or video distribution workflows because he hadn't, but he used lingo where appropriate to show he understood the concepts and the importance of the work he would be charged with doing.

Then he looked at his current experience through the lens of this opportunity. He connected the dots for the hiring manager (see the underlines on the lingo he used): He was part of a huge operation and knew how to <u>organize massive amounts of inventory and information</u> through <u>inventory-tracking software</u>. He focused on his desire to work for a cutting-edge company, how he had to <u>learn from scratch the technology</u> he currently used, and that he had the <u>skill to learn any new technology</u>. He focused heavily on soft skills such as working under <u>tight deadlines, solving problems as they arose, and adapting quickly to change</u> because productions and directions were fluid. Most importantly, he gave no indication of being desperate to leave his current role, emphasizing instead how his experience laid the foundation for this new role. His attitude and passion, combined with his ability to use the lingo of the job and connect the dots of multiple skill sets for the hiring manager, landed him the job, and he has since been converted to a staff employee.

No matter what you've done, you have skills. Look at them through the lens of the new career. You will be surprised at just how valuable they will be in the new career. You will bring something to the role that others will not—a unique perspective. Now you just need to find that perspective and hone your message.

Chapter 5 Summary

1. **Learn the lingo:** Research the language and concepts used in the new career and understand what they mean strategically and tactically.

2. **Connect skills:** Identify specific tasks in your past jobs, internships, and volunteer activities that would directly relate to the role you want simply by changing the lingo.

3. **Determine a unique perspective:** Determine how your experience from previous internships, volunteer activities, or jobs gives you a unique perspective for excelling at the new job.

4. **Hone your message:** Connect the dots on your resume and in interviews and adjust as you learn what is and isn't working in telling your story.

6

Recruiters Are the Gateway

"You can't knock on opportunity's door and not be ready."
—Bruno Mars, singer, songwriter, producer

You see a job that is perfect for you. You know you can do it. You apply online and attach your resume and cover letter and expect a call in the next week or so. Silence. You wait. Silence. And then, a few weeks or months later, you get the dreaded rejection email.

> *Unfortunately, we have decided not to proceed with your candidacy for the opening at Company. Hiring for this position is extremely competitive, and the candidate pool was very impressive. However, at this time, we have found a candidate who fulfills more requirements for the position.*

Not even a call or a personal email. What happened? What happened is your resume probably wasn't even looked at. That's right.

IT. WASN'T. EVEN. LOOKED. AT.

Let that sink in.

First, who is looking at your resume? Recruiters. Hiring managers rarely look at resumes until recruiters flag the ones that are most relevant. That means your target audience is recruiters, which may also be called "Staffing" or "Talent Acquisition" leaders. For the purposes of this chapter, I will stick with "recruiters."

It's important to understand the world of recruiters so you know who you are talking to and you understand how they work. There are two kinds of recruiters: internal and external recruiters. Each of those categories may include a specialized subcategory such as executive recruiters.

Types of Recruiters and How to Leverage Them

Internal Recruiters

Internal recruiters work inside a specific company and recruit for their employer (i.e., a recruiter who works at Google or Amazon and recruits only for that company). This type of recruiter has deep relationships with hiring managers and a deep understanding of the company culture because the recruiter works full-time inside the company. In many companies, this type of recruiter usually has a specialty such as general and administrative (legal, HR, marketing, finance—any part of a company that isn't R&D) or R&D (engineering, data science, and other technical-type roles). In a start-up environment, internal recruiters may recruit for everything because there may only be one or two.

External Recruiters

External recruiters have contracts with multiple companies to fill jobs. They are hired for many reasons, such as when companies don't have internal recruiters because a company is too small, or internal recruiters have exhausted their search and the company needs an outside recruiter to target the right talent pool. External recruiters, either independent or with an agency, will sometimes specialize in the services they offer so they know the talent pool deeply in one or two industries. For example, The Winford Group is known as one of the premier companies for recruiting business and legal affairs talent for studios, production companies, and entertainment companies, but it has also branched out into finance, marketing, creative, studio heads, and C-suite.

Executive Recruiters

Executive recruiters can be internal or external. They seek out experienced and established executives to fill senior-level roles, which are not always offered to the public. They may recruit for one industry or work across multiple industries. An example of an external executive recruiting agency would be Egon Zehnder or Spencer Stuart, which specialize in executive, CEO, and board advisory positions. Internal executive recruiters may recruit for vice presidents or above as well. Jane Ashen Turkewitz is the founder and managing director at Hi-Touch Search, specializing in recruiting high-level executives (director and above) for media and digital technology, and also worked as the deputy director of the University of Texas at Austin's NYC-based internship and experiential learning program, where she helped students secure internships.

Recruiters Don't Work for You

No matter what kind of recruiter you are talking to, they don't work for you; they work for companies. Alissa Block from The Winford Group says it best: "When I got into this business, I was a humanitarian and thought my mission was to help people find jobs. Hello, I cannot find people jobs! I feel horrible knowing and thinking this and horrible that I'm saying it out loud, but my job is not about finding jobs for people. It's about finding the best talent for the client hiring me to do a search for them. It's capitalism."

All recruiters want to work with top candidates because placing one in a new role means they get paid. When a recruiter is engaging and encouraging and makes you feel special, they are selling you on the company and the job while determining if you are a good fit for the role and the company culture. That's why there's an old saying that goes, "You may never be treated as well by an employer as you were treated the first time you talked to a recruiter."

Some recruiters are lifelong relationship builders. Alissa says she has more than 15,000 people in her database! She's not alone. Jane Turkewitz started recruiting in digital in 1999 before digital was even a thing. Now, more than twenty years later, she has a huge database of senior-level people in both digital and emerging media. And since many executives she has placed in digital media jobs have been interested in moving into the cannabis industry, she's been able to transfer into that space as well.

When Jane is working to fill a position, she may present two or three candidates to an employer. "I'm working with three candidates right now for one role. They all bring something different to the table, and the client will need to make a decision. Two of those people will be disappointed, but I don't just disappear and dump them. They are now in my network, and I will keep them in mind for future opportunities because they were professional throughout the entire process."

Jane says college graduates need to focus on maintaining and building relationships with *internal* recruiters at companies early in their career. For example, Jane describes one student who was interested in a position at a PR firm and was very active with an "early careers" recruiter with whom she built a rapport and had a great interview. The student was excited when she was told she would move to the next step in the process. But a month later, she received an offer from another company and accepted it. Jane explains that the student made a critical mistake when she accepted that offer before calling the PR firm. "The PR firm she desperately wanted to work for didn't move quick enough, which happens. But if she really wanted the job at that firm, she should have reached out to tell the recruiter she received another offer, but the PR firm was her first choice and could they expedite their process." Even worse, Jane explains, the student never reached out to the recruiter to thank her for everything she did. The recruiter saw the new graduate post her new job on LinkedIn and even sent a note saying she was thrilled for her but disappointed. The student never wrote back! Jane says, "That was another huge mistake. The student treated this like a transactional process instead of building a relationship for the future. If someone takes the time to nurture a relationship with you regardless of whether they were able to move you forward in the process, don't make it transactional."

Recruiters are always seeking people for new openings. Also, some recruiters move jobs just like employees move jobs. Relationships are everything in the business world, so even if a recruiter works for a company you don't have an interest in now, consider the future and where that recruiter may be as they move up in their own career.

How Recruiters Work

Most recruiters don't have time to look at every resume in an applicant tracking system (ATS)—an online system for applying for an open position. Internal recruiters I spoke to said they usually look at the first fifty resumes in an ATS. If there is no viable talent in that pool of resumes, they will look at the next few dozen applicants. They rarely look through the entire applicant pool unless the pool is low or the company has full-time resume screeners, which is not that common. External recruiters I spoke to will start with their own databases first. If they don't have any viable candidates, they will reach out to their contacts or post and/or search on LinkedIn.

Every recruiter is working on filling numerous roles at one time, so they look at resumes of new candidates very quickly. "Look" means that a recruiter *scans* a resume for mere seconds. Literally. In a 2018 eye-tracking study,[1] the job search site Ladders.com revealed that recruiters screen a resume for an average of seven seconds. That's higher than a previous study in 2012, which said they screened resumes for six seconds. Whoopee. Bob Hancock, who has been recruiting for more than twenty years and has managed teams of recruiters, says most positions receive at least a hundred resumes and many have more than five hundred applicants. There is no chance of spending quality time on a resume. "If you can't project who you are and what experience you have so I can be intrigued to look at it longer than ten seconds, then your resume isn't projecting your value."

When Jane looks at resumes from college students who are applying for internships, she can tell instantly if they understand that their resume is a marketing tool. "Your resume is not about you; it's about what you can do for the company. Resumes don't get you the job. They get you to the interview. So, your resume has to stand out like a brochure selling yourself. It needs to be customized to get someone to buy into your skillset because if you don't do that, there are a hundred more people behind you who can and will put in that effort."

Alissa from The Winford Group says she doesn't even post positions online because of all the resumes that don't match the job description. She reviews resumes from referrals for less than five seconds and from that says she can determine what brand name companies they worked for, what titles they've had, and whether their career trajectory was linear or took some twists and turns. "I honestly can't tell you if I have ever read a resume word for word. I scan straight down to the bottom and come back up."

I talked to dozens of recruiters and these three represent the consensus of most recruiters out there. Therefore, you have seconds to make an impression and show you have the right skills for the role, your career path and job-move timeline makes sense, you have industry and/or practical experience and/or transferable skills, and you are worthy of a phone call.

How Recruiters Find You

If recruiters don't already have a perfect entry-level candidate in mind from previous internships at the company or from a referral, some will post job descriptions or do a LinkedIn post explaining the opportunity and asking for referrals or applications. But not all perfect candidates are looking for a new role. So, recruiters will also seek "passive" candidates who may not be actively looking to make a move but might be interested if they hear about a great opportunity. Recruiters mainly use LinkedIn, while some pay for access to Indeed, Monster, Google, and other job search sites for entry and early career-level candidates. No matter the source, most recruiters do a Boolean search on LinkedIn using a string of hard skills that are critical to the job such as "SQL" or "salesforce" or "revenue recognition." Their search will yield hundreds of potential candidates, some with the exact skills they are looking for and some with only a few. What you don't know is recruiters can also see three important things when searching LinkedIn:

1. **Candidates who've already applied:** Internal recruiters can identify from LinkedIn who has already applied to the job

online through the company's applicant tracking system (ATS). If an external recruiter posts the role, then they can see who applied to their posting. Internal recruiters will first start looking at candidates found in their Boolean search who have already applied for the role because those candidates have already shown a proactive interest and will be easier to recruit. Further, jobs for entry-level or early-in-career roles have so many applicants, recruiters rarely need to hunt for candidates and can merely set a search in the ATS.

2. **A candidate's openness to new opportunities:** Recruiters can also see which LinkedIn profiles are set to "Open to New Opportunities" either publicly with the green banner or privately in the settings. As an early-in-career candidate, doing both is fine! If you haven't checked your LinkedIn settings for a while, at the very least, click on your picture (in the right corner next to notifications) and scroll down to Settings & Privacy. Make sure your Job Seeking Preferences are set in a way to be found along with your preference for location, and if you know, include desired industry, company size, and so on. This takes the guesswork out of what you want in your first job and allows recruiters to find you faster. Note: If you are currently working, while LinkedIn tries to prevent people at your current employer from seeing if your LinkedIn profile is set to "Open to New Opportunities," it doesn't promise that someone won't find out. I checked with recruiters at my company when I was looking for a new role and they couldn't see that my profile setting was open. But if one of their friends sees it and tells them, it's possible your boss could find out as well.

3. **The likelihood of a candidate responding to an inquiry:** Recruiters can determine who is more likely to respond to their LinkedIn emails based on a candidate's previous emails and responses to other inquiries. Recruiters can't see what you wrote to other recruiters, but an algorithm will tell them

whether you are more likely to respond if recruiters reach out. A former manager once told me, "Even if you are happy in your job, take every call or at least return every email." That's a lot of work if you are working and/or attending school full time. But there are reasons why you should take the time to do this:

➔ You want the recruiter to know who you are even if the current job being pitched isn't the right role for you based on your interests. As previously stated, internal recruiters change jobs just like you! You never know where that recruiter will be in a year or two or three.

➔ You can practice honing your message on every call.

Now you know how recruiters find you, but how do you make a recruiter look at your resume or LinkedIn profile for more than seven seconds and take the next step and call you?

Mastering the Applicant Tracking System

When you apply online, whether through LinkedIn, other job postings, or directly on a company's website, you are applying to an ATS if you aren't using email. It's the technology recruiters use to keep track of applicants and move them through the interview and hiring process. If you think of it as a place to apply for a single job, you are forgetting that every time you apply for a job at the same company, it stores your information.

So, if you apply for more than one role at a company or you are pursuing more than one career option, you need to have multiple resumes. But keep in mind the ATS will show the recruiter all the jobs you've applied for and all the versions of your resume if you are tailoring it to a particular role. If those jobs are completely different, such as in finance or marketing, then it looks like you don't know what you want to do and are applying for anything and everything without a focus. That's a huge red flag for recruiters. Jane sees people sending resumes to every opening they find and multiple openings at the same company. "Candidates are making a big mistake by spraying and praying with their resumes. You must be strategic on what you go for because we get so many resumes. If you don't specify and customize your resume to the specs in the job description, you won't get any traction."

Therefore, if your experience translates to more than one role in different fields, don't apply for both of them at the same company. The exception to this is if you know someone at the company who believes your skills could be a great fit for multiple roles and is willing to champion you through the recruiting process.

In addition to recruiters, companies will use AI programs to search resumes for key words in the job description. This is another critical skill to master.

Make Transferable Skills Noticeable

Job seekers often read a job description, know they can do the job, and have all the requisite experience, yet never receive that call. Why? They probably didn't tailor their resume with the right key words. If you are looking for your first job, you have to work even harder to show you are the right person for a role you've never done before. Your resume and LinkedIn profile may be your first impression and needs to be discovered in a recruiter's Boolean search. Therefore, they must include at least 75% of the hard skills listed in the job description in clear, concise sentences. For example:

Posted job description:

Company A is looking to hire a staff accountant to work in the SaaS-based industry, whose duties will be matching invoices to purchase orders/vouchers, processing accounts payable (A/P) and accounts receivable (A/R), and assisting in month-end.

Resume bullet point:

- Worked with senior staff accountants in meticulously matching invoices to purchase order/vouchers and processing accounts payable (A/P) and accounts receivable (A/R) in alignment with closing books at the month and year end.

This person doesn't say she processes accounts payables or accounts receivables but uses the key words from the job description to show that she has an understanding and has some experience with those concepts. By using "key words," it is more likely her LinkedIn profile will pop up in a Boolean search. Showing transferable skills and using key words are critical to being found. An entire chapter (chapter 9) is dedicated to highlighting transferable skills from any job, internship, or volunteer activity.

Find a Connection to the Role or Company

Once you have applied online, don't expect a recruiter to review your resume unless you've made sure they see it. As previously stated, recruiters don't review every resume in the ATS. Since recruiters only look at the first fifty resumes, if you are applicant 125, your resume may never be viewed, even if it perfectly aligns to the role. That's why it's so important to contact a professional colleague in the company and the recruiter directly. If you can see the recruiter who posted the role on LinkedIn, apply through the link provided and then email the recruiter to tell them you applied to the role and why you are a perfect fit. Both Bob and Jane say they appreciate it if a candidate reaches out to them directly, as long as they reach out appropriately.

If you can't see which recruiter posted the position, start searching for a connection. On LinkedIn, see if you have mutual connections with others. If you don't have an obvious connection and you are applying for, say, a marketing job, do a LinkedIn or a Google search for "marketing, company name, recruiter name." If their profile says something like, "Staffing marketing roles at [company name]," you've probably found the right person. If you find recruiters at the company you are applying to, but their profiles don't distinguish which specific area they recruit for, send them a LinkedIn message anyway because there's a good chance the one you found will pass along your information if your resume shows directly applicable skills.

If you can't find the recruiter, try to find someone at the company you know or a colleague who knows someone there. If it is a specific job within a field like "product marketing," do a LinkedIn search for "product marketing, company name" under LinkedIn People. You may find a director or senior director who could be the hiring manager, or search for a VP or SVP who may be the head of the department. Then see if you know anyone who knows that person. You can always send a LinkedIn message directly to the potential hiring manager in a specific area, but without a connection, that random communication may not elicit a response. Referrals are always the best way to be noticed by a recruiter and/or the hiring manager.

How to Approach a Recruiter

Approaching a recruiter can start a beautiful relationship or make a recruiter never want to talk to you again. Recruiters are usually filling more than a dozen roles at any one time. Your first email, resume, and/ or LinkedIn profile must be perfectly aligned to the role you are applying for and it must be easy to read or you may never get a response. Look at your communication to a recruiter from their perspective. If they spent all day responding to every person who applied, no jobs would ever be filled! So only reach out if:

1. You have the right recruiter for your field. Reaching out to recruiters is fine if you know you are targeting the right recruiter for your field. If you find one who hasn't posted a role but works in the field in which you are seeking a position, reach out and introduce yourself. But if you are seeking a role in finance, don't reach out to a recruiter who only specializes in marketing (unless you acknowledge to the recruiter they are at the company you want to work for but realize they may not be the recruiter for this position).

When you do reach out, be extremely specific about why. Here's a great example:

Hi [recruiter name],

I'm reaching out because I am seeking a marketing role where I can bring value. Here is the type of role I'm seeking:

Position—Full-time employee. Open to full-time contract work.

Title—Entry Level/Associate: marketing associate, marketing specialist.

Location—Open to anywhere in the country.

Industries—Technology, software and hardware, AI, cybersecurity, cryptocurrency, med-tech.

Company—Prefer smaller company (under 5,000 employees) but open for right opportunity. Start-ups okay.

Compensation—Negotiable.

My resume is attached for your review. I look forward to hearing from you when you have a position where you think I could bring the most value.

Sincerely,

[your name]

Never reach out and say, "Hi, here's my resume if you have something," or "If you hear of anything, please let me know," or one of Jane's favorites: "I was wondering if you would share my resume with your network because I am looking for a new job in [specific field]." NO! Never email a recruiter this way. First, you are asking someone you don't know to champion you without them knowing if you would be a good employee. Second, you are asking someone else to do your job search. You need to build the relationship. Your only thought should be how you can help a recruiter fill a specific role. You may never hear back if there isn't an opening, but you never know if that same recruiter will have a future opening and remember reading your note.

2. The recruiter has posted a job that matches your overall skill set.
If you see a post that is perfect for your skill set, your resume is ready and your message is clear, and you have already applied online, you can alert the recruiter to your interest through a LinkedIn message. Example:

Hi [recruiter name],

I recently applied for [title of job (include job number if applicable)] at [company name]. I believe I would be able to bring great value to the role.

I have attached my resume for your review. I hope to have the opportunity to connect with you to discuss my skills, experience, and passion for [key requirements of the job from the job description such as "creating marketing campaigns which engage audiences."].

Best,

[your name]

Even though the recruiter can review your LinkedIn profile and can find your resume in the ATS, attach it again for convenience. Again, you may never receive a response, but if you don't send a message, you are leaving it up to chance whether your resume will be seen at all.

Say No to Gimmicks

When I was applying for my first job, I was told to use a gimmick like sending chocolate with my resume or attaching my resume to a pizza box. Back in 1992, the country was coming out of a recession, so jobs weren't easy to find. I did try, and not one of my "gimmicks" worked. And yet today, thirty years later, I've seen these same gimmicks and many others from people hoping to catch a recruiter's attention. Recruiters have reported gimmicks such as receiving a resume with shoes in a shoebox from a candidate trying to "get his foot in the door," to getting donuts with a note saying, "Donut miss this opportunity to interview me." Sure, recruiters and staff may chuckle at how "funny" the gesture was, but rarely will a candidate receive a call no matter how original the gimmick. They can look desperate and silly and make a recruiter feel uncomfortable. A gimmick will never advance your candidacy. Most recruiters enjoy the laugh but then move on. Therefore, save your money or spend it on a resume writer if you need help attracting recruiters' attention.

Even in the world of "viral" media, you will end up realizing that it wasn't the gimmick as much as the relationships that worked. You may have read about a Silicon Valley homeless man, David Cesarez, who put on a shirt and tie and stood on a busy road with a sign, "Homeless, hungry 4 success. Take a resume." A person took his picture and posted it on Twitter. It immediately went viral; he received more than two hundred job offers, and he accepted a job at White Fox Defense.[2] The reason his stunt went viral wasn't only because he was standing on a road in a suit and tie but because his resume was clear, showing his experience and professionalism.[3] Further, when he interviewed for the job, he was prepared to discuss his experience and the value he could bring to a company. Based on his Twitter message about landing the job, it appears that numerous people rallied behind him to help him land at White Fox—people he had built relationships with. While he was "found" on the side of the road, in the end, his relationships were instrumental in him landing a job, not the gimmick.

Relationships with Recruiters

A final note about your relationship with recruiters. You are rarely the only applicant in play. In an effort to sell a candidate on a job and a company, recruiters are friendly, listen, and work hard to excite you about an opportunity. But since they aren't working for you, you are likely not the only person they are talking to no matter how perfect or enthusiastic you are for the role. Why? Because the company may not meet your salary needs, you may be a wrong culture fit, you may not make it through the interview process with the hiring manager or other interviewers, or you may simply be the second-best candidate for reasons you are not privy to. If you are a #2, stay in touch with the recruiter and/or the hiring manager because you may be a #1 in the future. That's what happened to me at Intuitive. After multiple rounds of interviews, I was rejected for the first role I applied for simply because someone else was a better fit for that client group, but days later the recruiter reached back out and had another opportunity to discuss. That opportunity became my next job. Recruiters may not technically work for you, but they are certainly your most important relationship when trying to land your next role.

Chapter 6 Summary

1. **Types of recruiters:** Know what type of recruiter you are talking to—internal, external, executive—and understand their role in the hiring process.

2. **Make yourself easy to find:** Create an open pathway to recruiters by opening up your LinkedIn profile to new opportunities, responding to all inquiries even if you aren't interested, and applying to all jobs that interest you as soon as you see the opening.

3. **Make your skills noticeable:** Use key words from job descriptions on LinkedIn and in your resume.

4. **Find connections:** Once you have applied online, look for direct or indirect connections to the posted position or company and reach out to the recruiter (if known) or anyone who can refer you to the role.

7

Resume Formatting

"Simple can be harder than complex: You have to work hard to get your thinking clean to make it simple. But it's worth it in the end because once you get there, you can move mountains."

—Steve Jobs, Apple co-founder

Fancy colors, divider lines, cool shapes, shading, and formatting with Employment, Education, and Skills in one column and the rest of your experience in the other. You spend hours making your resume look "pretty," and yet no one is calling you. That's because your resume either has no applicable substance to the job description, the message wasn't clear, you had typos or grammatical mistakes, or that pretty formatting was messed up in the applicant tracking system and you didn't manually input the information when you applied.

Keep It Simple

Recruiters and hiring managers don't care about fancy pictures or formatting. Even if you are interested in a creative field such as graphic design, your experience will speak for itself in your portfolio. The overall format simply needs to be clean with enough white space for balance, easily scanned, and contain information that convinces a recruiter you have the experience and skills for the role. Remember: recruiters review resumes for an average of seven

Tip #7: Simple, clean resume format is the best format.

seconds, so they aren't actually reading it; they are looking for key skills that match the job description.

The first step is to get out of your head. Creating a resume that attracts attention causes anxiety because a lot rides on it, and you can get caught up in how to format it. What goes first, education or experience? How many pages should it be? Should I add color and a design? Before digging into the best way to highlight transferable skills on your resume, let's get the basic formatting questions out of the way. You can find some answers online or in resume books, but it always amazes me how often the most professional and high-level executives can't format their resume in a way that reflects their strengths and skills in an easy-to-read format. So, don't skip this chapter!

Basic Formatting

AI programs such as ChatGPT or resume-building features in Microsoft, Canva, or other programs are fine to use. But, the best way to leverage them is to build your resume first with your experience and accomplishments, then ask the AI program to edit it or make your bullet points under each job more dynamic. While building your resume, keep these formatting tips in mind:

1. How many pages? More pages will not equate to more experience or make your resume "better." I like to use "the rule of ten": If you have more than ten years' experience after college and multiple employers, you may have a two-page resume. If you have less than ten years' experience after college graduation, no matter how many internships, jobs, or volunteer activities you have, your resume should be one page. The goal is to fill it up with substantive information but not a laundry list of every possible task or accomplishment. Resumes should only show the specific experiences and/or skills that are relevant to the job you're applying for.

2. White space. White space in a resume is critical. That means you need a proper header and footer (no less than .6 inch in Microsoft Word) and white space on both sides of your resume (no less than .7 inch) for nice clean margins. The middle of your resume should have proper spacing of at least one space or 1.5 spaces between each subject section (e.g., between the end of the Experience section and the start of the Education section) and between each job, which can be slightly less. In short, the resume should be easy to glance at, not read.

3. Font. Calibri, Arial Narrow, and Candara are all fine. Arial tends to take up more space if you need to fill up your resume while Calibri, Candara, or Arial Narrow are smaller. Stay away from cursive (Lucinda) or fancy-looking (Harrington) fonts. No one cares what font you use as long as it's consistent throughout your resume and easy to read. Font size should never be less than 11 point for the main content. For headers, consider 14 or 16 if you have room.

4. Grammar/punctuation. Using proper grammar and punctuation is obviously important. If you don't know how to use a semicolon, don't (and I find that most people *don't* know how to use it!). Given today's emphasis on email and texting, we write more than we talk, and so if you aren't a good writer or English is a second language, ask a friend or hire someone to rewrite and/or review your resume. You can also use Grammarly, which reviews and edits your writing, grammar, and punctuation and can spice up commonly used verbs and adjectives. It can also provide input on the tone of your cover letter. As for bullet points of success and roles under a job title, some people write sentence fragments, which don't require periods. I personally like periods at the end of each bullet point. The choice is yours; just be consistent.

5. Color. Should you highlight some words in color, like your name or job titles? You can, but it's optional. Find one that is pleasing on the eyes and bold but not startling. Red is startling and also hard to read. Some blues are too bright. Color should be used sparingly and, again, consistently. If you highlight one job title, make sure all of them are the same color.

6. Capitals, bold, underlines. There are no rules about what and how to emphasize something, but too many emphases can clutter a resume. Be discerning and be consistent. If you boldface the title of your job on one line, then do it with every job title. If you underline the company you work for, you should underline every previous company.

7. Chronological or skills based. Always default to a chronological resume because it will always translate better in an ATS and it clearly shows your career history and path. That said, most ATSs allow you to both input the data chronologically and attach a skills-based resume if that's a better way to showcase your transferrable skills. Consider using a skills-based resume if you don't have a lot of work experience but you have gained skills that are relevant to your chosen career; you've had internships, jobs, or volunteer activities in which you did the same work in each one and the core skills gained are the same (e.g., TV news reporting); or there is no other way to highlight transferable skills from previous work, volunteer, or internship experience.

Chronological resumes should show work experience in descending order with the most current job at the top and each prior job following in order by date. Some people have multiple freelance jobs. The one that is most current or most relevant to the job you're applying for should be first. Also, some people have a "volunteer activity" that is more relevant than their internships. Whether you are paid for a job or work full-time or part-time doesn't matter when it comes to order of experience. The most relevant experience with the most current date that showcases applicable skills should always be first.

8. Home address. There is no reason to include your address on your resume. In Los Angeles, if you live in Silver Lake but apply for a job in Santa Monica, putting your address on your resume may exclude you when the recruiter thinks about commuting time. You don't want a recruiter to make that decision for you before you've had a chance to explain how you love long commutes or would be willing to move closer for the role. Further, if a job doesn't include relocation expense support, you may be dismissed even if you were willing to move on your own. What if your cell phone number is Los Angeles but you want to show you live in San Francisco where the position is located? How will a recruiter know you don't need a relocation package? Put the city/state next to each role; your most recent or current role should say, for example, "San Francisco, CA." If you've moved home or to a specific location after graduation and only want to work in that location, then you can add city and state to your resume header with your email and phone number.

9. Name, email, phone, and social media.

Name: If your name is Robert and you go by Bobby, put Bobby on your resume and on your LinkedIn profile. When you apply online and fill in ATS information, enter Robert and, under Nickname, Bobby. If your nickname is "cute" like Sweetpea, use your real name. And make sure that your name is a bigger font size than the rest of the resume. It doesn't need to be 72, but at least 16.

Email: Your email should also be professional. Don't use your high school "fun" address, such as bigdog@xxxx.com or sexyAlexa@xxxx .com, which doesn't show workplace maturity. Also, don't use your college email address even if you haven't graduated, because you want to show you have "moved on" to a professional email. Finally, consider creating an email address just for job searching so you won't miss any critical emails that come in. Recruiters often reach out via email first to see if you respond and to coordinate a time to speak.

Phone: This should be your cell phone. Don't worry if the prefix is from a different city/state where you currently live. Mobility is common these days and recruiters don't worry about the number they are calling to reach you.

Social media: Include a hyperlink to your LinkedIn profile, using the word "LinkedIn" Or "LinkedIn Profile." The only time you would add Instagram, Facebook, or other platforms is when you are applying for a job that requires social media use (e.g., marketing) or savvy. But be careful! Make sure your social media (even if private) is not full of pictures of you drinking, posing provocatively, or making comments which can be judged as distasteful.

Putting It All Together

All contact information should be on the second line or grouped together. You don't have to write "email" and then write your email or "phone" before your phone number. However, you can separate them by a symbol like a circle, square, or diamond. Add a hyperlink to your LinkedIn profile. Here are two examples:

First & Last Name
myname@gmail.com • 310-555-5555 • LinkedIn

---

or

First & Last Name
myname@gmail.com ◆ 310-555-5555 ◆ LinkedIn

Contact information can also be grouped on the right if it's clean and readable:

First & Last Name   myname@gmail.com
310-555-5555
LinkedIn

---

10. The line. It's nice to put a divider line under your contact information. Whether you do a single, double, thick, thin—it's your choice! And it's fine not to have one.

11. Full-perimeter page borders. Not necessary, but if you want one, go right ahead.

12. "Legally eligible" to work in the United States. When you apply online, the applicant tracking system will ask this question. That said, if you have a concern that you may not be considered for a role because your name is unique, your internship or volunteer experience is mostly outside the US, or your last job was outside the US, it doesn't hurt to add the words "Legally eligible to work in the United States" along with your contact information. Examples:

First & Last Name
myname@gmail.com • 310-555-5555 • LinkedIn
Legally eligible to work in the United States

---

or

First & Last Name   myname@gmail.com
                                          310-555-5555
                                          LinkedIn
Legally eligible to work in the United States

---

13. Objective vs. summary. Your resume should start with a strong statement of who you are. This is not an objective; your objective is to get a job. And don't title it with "Summary" or anything else that is redundant to the statement. It should relate directly to the job you are applying for using key words from the job description; it is not a generic statement about what you've accomplished. How to craft such an opening will be explored in the next chapter. A formatting example looks like this:

First & Last Name
myname@gmail.com • 310-555-5555 • LinkedIn

PRODUCT MARKETING SPECIALIST with a blend of technical, business, and marketing skills who engages customers through designing and implementing innovative go-to-market strategies, sales initiatives, and campaigns across all verticals.

---

14. Core skills. Listing the applicable core hard and soft skills you've gained that are needed for the role from the keywords in the job description will help a recruiter recognize that you understand what is needed in the position. For example, here is a core-skills section for an entry-level social media specialist:

Core Skills

► Google analytics certified	► Content activations
► Creative storytelling	► Community engagement
► Content creation	► Final Cut Pro
► Brand advocacy	► Adobe Illustrator
► Social channel distribution	► Adobe Photoshop
► Product launches	► Adobe After Effects

This section can also focus more on soft skills or a combination of hard and soft skills for someone who doesn't have a lot of work experience.

Core Skills

► Creative storyteller	► Quick learner
► Collateral developer	► Detail oriented
► Self-starter	► Team player
► Analytical thinker	► Customer oriented
► Effective communicator	

These examples show the core skills in a section near the top of a resume but can also be captured in a left column on a resume. Applicants who want one resume to capture expertise for similar roles with slightly different skills (e.g., brand marketing roles and product marketing roles) may want to list all core skills in a separate column down the left side of a resume so the resume can be tailored slightly per application.

15. Experience. Which comes first, the job title or company name where you work (or worked)? Lead with the company name if

→ the company you worked, interned, or volunteered for is prominent like Google, RCA Records, or Make-A-Wish Foundation.

→ the company you are applying to is a direct competitor or comparable to the company where you have gained some experience.

→ you don't have any previous titles that are similar or related to the career you are pursuing or there is no way to adjust previous titles to make them directly relevant (see more below).

→ you've had multiple titles at any one company (from promotions or changing roles) even if that company isn't wholly relevant to the job you are pursuing. For example, you worked at a grocery store to pay for college and you started as a checker, then moved to bakery manager, then store assistant manager. This shows leadership and is relevant to any new career.

Example of how it should look:

IBM, Armonk, NY
Marketing Specialist

Start with your title if none of the above are true *and*

→ the companies you have worked for are not well known to the average person.

→ your previous job titles with the word "Intern" or "Volunteer" or "Freelancer" after them are the same or similar job titles to the job title of the position open.

→ you have created a company for providing freelance work and your title is the same or similar to the job titles you are pursuing.

Examples would be:

Social Media Marketing Intern
IBM, Armonk, NY

or

Marketing Specialist
JS Marketing LLC, Jennison, TN

The second example demonstrates how freelance work under your own company could be displayed on your resume.

Title: If your title doesn't match the job you are applying for, you can change it slightly to make it relevant. My title at Viacom was VP, Business and Legal Affairs, Labor and Employment, Production Risk Team. It was too long to put on a resume and would not have been directly relevant to the HR business partner roles I was applying for. Most recruiters would have dismissed me as "just a lawyer." But I was a business partner every day to leaders at all levels in the company, so I shortened it to "Production Risk Business Partner," which captured the essence of the work. When asked if I worked in HR, my answer was clear: "No. I report up through the legal department, but I work as a business partner to leaders throughout the organization cross-functionally, including . . ." Be careful not to cross the line into a lie.

Multiple titles, same company: If you have been promoted at any job or internship, fantastic! That shows you have grown in previous roles. In that case, the company will always be first so you can list your numerous jobs under it:

Bobbledeboo, Inc., Jennison, TN	5/21–8/23
Sr. Marketing Intern (promoted)	5/22–8/23
Marketing Intern	5/21–8/21

Temp work for a company through a third-party agency: If you work as a temporary worker or as a freelance worker, you may go to one company every day for work but you are truly employed through a third party. Use the actual employer (the agency) in the ATS but list the company(ies) that benefited from your work on your resume:

Social Media Intern	5/22–8/23
Bobbledeboo, Inc. through ABC Agency	

Dates of employment: There is no right way to format dates, but they should go on the right-hand side as shown above and should not be bold or underlined. Dates provide two pieces of data: How many years' experience you have in a specific area and/or whether you change jobs often. Your work history should dictate how you format your dates.

Standard dates include month/year such as 6/2020–6/2024 or 6/20–6/24 for someone who is employed. You can also use spelled-out months if you like that look better: September 2022–June 2024. If you have a long title, you may need to use the shortest date format. Either way, be consistent with use of hyphens or dashes between dates. Whichever date format you choose, be consistent throughout your resume.

Experience timeline: If you worked in high school and, in addition, have college internships or other experience that is relevant to the new job, you will need to determine whether to include your high school experience on your resume. There is no hard rule for this. Consider how relevant the experience is to the career you want to pursue, and whether you can provide bullet points that demonstrate relevant skills. If it is not relevant, but you don't have a lot of other experience through internships or volunteer activities, you can include it to show you have some work experience. That said, if you have more relevant experience through internships, freelance work, or volunteer activities, then you can leave off high school work experience.

Bullet points vs. paragraphs. All resumes should have bullet points under the job title/company. Some resumes also feature a sentence under each job title describing the business or the overall nature of the job.

> **Bobbledeboo, Inc.,** Jennison, TN   6/22–Current
> Marketing Specialist
> Fast-growing startup that connects mission-based advertisers with platform opportunities.

A descriptor sentence is fine if the company isn't well known and you want to relate it to the company you are applying to (e.g., you are relating the above job to a job opening at a digital advertising company). You may also use that brief statement as a quick summary of your applicable skills. That said, I don't recommend it and believe the "type of company" you work for can fit within the first bullet point. Extra lines mean extra reading. Your experience is more critical than what your company sold or whether it's in the Fortune 500. For example:

Bobbledeboo, Inc., Jennison, TN   6/22–Current
Marketing Intern

▸ Engaged with customers on social channels, including Instagram, Facebook, LinkedIn, TikTok, X, and Threads, to foster a positive and supportive community through addressing customer concerns and questions in a timely and empathetic manner for this advertising platform company.

How many bullet points should each job have? At least three bullet points for jobs that are less than ten years old. Further, each bullet point should start with an active verb (i.e., "Led," "Coordinated," "Assisted," "Drafted," or "Facilitated") instead of a passive one ("Responsible for").

Location: You may have noticed that the location of each job has fluctuated in the above examples between the top and second line. Sometimes it is next to the company and sometimes it's next to the job title. Again, there is no hard rule; it should go where it fits best. Location only communicates whether you are an in-state candidate or may require a relocation package, which is uncommon for early career professionals. For foreign nationals, it proves you are currently working in the US and legally eligible to work in the US.

16. Education. Education today means a lot less than it did just a few years ago. In late 2018, Glassdoor compiled a list of companies no longer requiring a college degree for certain high-level jobs, which included Apple, Penguin Random House, Google, Bank of America, Home Depot, and IBM. College is a great time to grow up, learn what you want to do, and gain some work experience, but companies are starting to realize that the right experience is as important as education, if not more so.

Going to an Ivy League school shows you either have the capacity to learn and the drive to succeed or your family has deep connections. (Not trying to insult!) That said, I firmly believe that education should come after experience. Experience gets you the job; education is more of a "connection" or a "talking point." Some people disagree with me on this; don't worry, your resume will not be rejected because you put education first. Here are some examples where that makes sense:

→ You are a recent graduate who went to a top-ten school such as Harvard, Yale, or Stanford. You have an exceptionally high GPA *and* you don't have a lot of relevant work experience. For example, you were on a work-study program to put yourself through school, so your resume is full of security or library intake jobs. Kudos to you. Work-study takes grit!

→ You went to a top school in your location, such as UC Berkeley near San Francisco or UCLA or USC in Los Angeles, and you are seeking work in the same city *but* you don't have a lot of relevant work experience.

→ You know someone at the company where you are applying who is an alumnus from your school *and* you have a high GPA (3.5 or above).

Education should always be listed with the school first followed by the degree underneath in descending chronological order:

University of California, Los Angeles   5/2024
Master of Business Administration, GPA 3.6

University of California, Los Angeles   5/2023
BA Communication, GPA 4.0

Again—and it's worth repeating—I firmly believe that education goes after experience on a resume even if you don't have much of a work history. Why? Because this book is teaching you how to make whatever experiences you do have relevant to the field you want to move into.

GPA. There is no reason to list your GPA unless it is above a 3.5 and you graduated in the past three years. Otherwise leave it off. Most companies don't care about GPA and if it is important, the recruiter will ask you for it.

Activities/Clubs. New graduates should only list activities if they are relevant to the type of jobs you are applying for and you need to fill your resume. All diversity clubs are relevant. If you played on a college sports team, that is relevant because it shows that you have a competitive spirit, understand discipline and the value of hard work. Clubs associated with "communication" are relevant because every job requires solid written and verbal communication. If your resume is already filled with internships, just list the name of the school and the degree and try to add keywords and relevant skills based on your involvement in clubs. For example, this person is applying for finance positions:

University of California, Los Angeles   May 2024
BA Communication

- ▸ Treasurer, Communications Club—Managed budget, and all finance and accounting including membership dues and accounts payable and receivable to ensure club operated within the annual budget.
- ▸ Volunteer, Big Buddy Mentor Program—Gained an appreciation for diversity and differences while mentoring special needs men and women in basic life skills, such as balancing a checkbook, paying a tip, and handling financial social interactions.
- ▸ Member, Omega Psi Phi Fraternity, Inc. (Black Law Student Association)—Participated in events that educated employers about diversity in the workplace.

17. Skills proficiencies. If you are creating a skills-based resume or if you are a new graduate or you don't have a "Skills" section or you haven't performed certain skills within your internships or volunteer activities, but you are proficient in them, list them at the end of your resume under the heading, "Additional Skills," "Skills Proficiencies," or just "Skills." For example:

Skills Proficiencies

▸ MS Office including Excel, Outlook, PowerPoint, One Note, Cloud
  Computing

Or if you are applying for a data science role:

Technical Proficiencies

▸ SQL, Python, Java, Scala, R, Julia, C++

18. Awards/published articles/blogs. Include these under the job or school where you received or published them. List only those published articles or awards that are directly applicable to the job you are applying for. Publishing articles on LinkedIn doesn't count unless that's a requirement of the prospective job. Blogging doesn't count unless it is part of the prospective job or the blog posts are relevant to the prospective job. These should not be listed in a separate section; better to fit them under the employer or school (just like your activities above) depending on when you published, unless you need to fill up space on your resume.

19. Hobbies/interests/volunteer work. These do not belong on a resume. In general, recruiters and hiring managers don't care whether you love to cook, like to travel, or are building your own tiny home. Outside hobbies mean you aren't focused on work. That said, if you are a marathoner who finished your twentieth marathon, or as mentioned, you were on a college athletic team (D1 or otherwise), then you may want to include that information because these show grit. If you have visited fifty countries to learn about cultural differences across the world or extensively traveled in one region (e.g., Asia), then include that because it will show your ability to work effectively with diverse team members. Otherwise, keep them to yourself unless they come up during the interview process. Volunteer work can be used as a job under "Experience" if that experience is more relevant with transferrable skills to the job you are applying to than any other experience on your resume. (More on this in chapter 10.)

What to *Not* Put on Your Resume

- → **Pictures.** Never put a picture of yourself on your resume. It can lead to unintentional bias by the recruiter or hiring manager. Also, it's just creepy. You're not dating; you're looking for a job! That's what LinkedIn is for and, yes, you should have a picture on LinkedIn.

- → **Tables, charts, diagrams, graphs, graphics, text boxes, icons.** The ATS will not interpret these correctly and could garble the rest of the information.

- → **First- or third-person sentences.** Never use "I," "she," "he," "me," or "my." Everyone knows it is your resume, so this is unnecessary. The only time you would use these is if you would like to put the gender pronoun you identify with next to your name.

- → **Proprietary/confidential information.** This could be anything such as sales-rate cards or company revenue. Use percentages instead (e.g., achieved 110% of goal).

- → **References.** Don't add reference contact information to a resume or "References Available Upon Request." Of course they are! Just have your references ready for when they ask you for them. (More on this in chapter 15).

- → **High school.** Don't list your high school unless you didn't go to college. If you don't have a bachelor's degree and the job requires it, leave education completely off your resume. If you started college but didn't finish, put the college on your resume and dates attended, but do not put the degree on your resume or it will be deceiving to the recruiter unless you add anticipated date of graduation.

Your resume or LinkedIn profile will be the very first interaction a recruiter has with you. Your resume should be neat, in the proper order, consistently formatted, and free of grammatical and spelling errors. Ask friends to look at it from a "format only" perspective to make sure it is easy to glance at for seven seconds. Then test your friend or a family member on what they learned from your resume in under ten seconds to make sure your message is clear. Once clear and full of substantive, relevant information, your resume will be ready to submit to a prospective job.

Chapter 7 Summary

1. **Keep it simple:** Don't add fancy fonts or a lot of color. The best resumes are simple and clean with a lot of white space.

2. **One or two pages:** Most college graduates should have a one page resume, but if you have extensive internships and job experience, it can be one-and-a-half or two pages. Never exceed two pages. Don't put every accomplishment on your resume—just the most relevant ones.

3. **Experience in descending order:** All jobs should be listed with the most current position first and the oldest last.

4. **Feature both hard and soft skills:** Add a core skills section that includes all the keywords from job descriptions in your field.

8

Setting Your Resume's Substantive Theme

"When I let go of what I am, I become what I might be."
—Lao Tzu, Chinese philosopher

Most people draft resumes based on their past experience and define themselves by their professional accomplishments. But you are reading this book because you don't want to look backward; you want to look forward toward your first professional career. Therefore, you should create your resume using the lens of the job you are applying for in the career you want to pursue. Since most college graduates have never worked in that new career as a full-time employee, the job description will be your guide.

Dissect the Job Description

Job descriptions hold the key to what is most important in your targeted position. Two companies may post the same title for a position, but the roles and responsibilities may be vastly different. For example, two people say, "I want a delicious fruit dessert." One asks for a slice of apple pie and the other wants a bowl of berries. Or one wants apple pie with a big scoop of vanilla ice cream and the other wants apple pie with extra cinnamon and nutmeg. When you read job descriptions, you need to identify the most important skills needed for the role and then design your resume according to the company's expectations and needs. A generic resume with everything you've ever done ignores the specific needs of the new job. It either won't be read or could be viewed

negatively by a recruiter who questions your focus or whether you have relevant skills. Once you find the positions you want, your mission is to determine who you are in relation to those job descriptions and present an alignment.

A summary of skills on your resume explains who you are professionally, what you can do, and how successful you are at doing it. It is about positioning your achievements through the lens of the new role so others can see how your unique skills are applicable. Also helpful is an introductory statement. While some recruiters may skip over this sentence, none have ever rejected a resume because it is there, and it can be a strategic opening. This sentence should grab the recruiter's attention and motivate them to read the rest of the resume. How do you craft a strong, authentic, opening statement defining who you are and what you can/want to do? Here are three easy steps:

1. Dissect the job description for hard and soft skills. Print out each job description and highlight all the relevant skills it emphasizes. Hard skills include actual experience such as SQL expertise or building marketing campaigns or specialized knowledge in a specific industry, such as biotech or gaming. Soft skills represent the "how" of a job such as "self-starter" and "able to work cross-functionally."

When reading the sample job description below, notice the **bold for hard skills**, <u>underline for soft skills</u>, and *italics* for words to potentially use in the cover letter:

<u>Product Marketing Associate</u>
[company] is looking for a hardcore **product marketing associate** to support our Director with the **design and implementation of go-to-market strategies** for our *industry-leading technology solutions*. You will help to establish [company's] position in the **SaaS industry** by **creating compelling market positioning and be responsible for helping**

the team create persuasive sales initiatives and campaigns ranging from cloud-connected messaging to vertical market solutions. You will also develop collateral from concept to publishing.

You must be a highly motivated and dedicated marketer and a self-starter who is comfortable in a *dynamic, fast-paced environment.* You must possess strong execution skills and enjoy being part of a team. You are expected to be a stellar communicator capable of learning our product and then engage customers and partners while evangelizing our product. This is a *high-visibility position* that requires a blend of technical, business, and marketing skills.

Once you've dissected the job description, you will have the information you need to highlight in your introductory statement. AI can also be helpful in identifying hard and soft skills. Input the job description into an AI program such as ChatGPT and ask it to generate all the hard and soft skills from the job description.

Title Yourself

2. **How do you want to "label" yourself?** There are many ways to start this first sentence, but if you look at the job description, the soft skills will give you the answer. In fact, you have choices: "highly motivated," "dedicated marketer," "self-starter," "team player," "stellar communicator." Characteristics such as "dedicated," "self-starter," "highly motivated," "team player," and "stellar communicator" could be used by anyone who believes those are applicable. The object is to find the strongest, legitimate version of you and lead your resume with those critical first words. Here are some examples for someone who has no experience or some internship experience:

→ **Highly motivated, detail-oriented self-starter . . .**
(Note that "detail oriented" is not in the above job description. That's fine! It's a great skill to have in any job.)

→ **"Highly motivated product marketing associate . . ."**

3. Incorporate hard and soft skills into your summary statement.
Incorporate all relevant hard skills from the job description into your summary. If you have little experience, focus on your soft skills but add a few hard skills. Here is an example for the new graduate with some internship experience in marketing (**bold** and <u>underlined</u> only to show correlating hard and soft skills respectively):

> <u>Highly motivated</u> **marketing associate** with a **blend of technical, business, and product marketing skills** who excels at **engaging customers, designing and implementing go-to-market strategies, and creating persuasive sales initiatives** and **campaigns.**

Grab Attention

The first sentence should grab a recruiter's attention. There is no perfect format, but the intent should be to make "who you are" and the skills you will bring stand out. Therefore, while there is no rule, consider highlighting the first few words in "SMALL CAPS" or "ALL CAPS" and/or making the font slightly bigger for those first few words. Such style changes will give your first sentence some pop and make it stick out. In the example below, the first few words are in CAPS AND SMALL CAPS at 13 point font size followed by plain 12 point font size.

First & Last Name
myname@gmail.com • 310-555-5555 • LinkedIn

HIGHLY MOTIVATED MARKETING ASSOCIATE with a blend of technical, business, and product marketing skills who excels at engaging customers, designing and implementing go-to-market strategies, and creating persuasive sales initiatives and campaigns.

After you write this sentence, own it. That is who you are, how you will characterize yourself in interviews, and how you will establish yourself in your chosen field. If you can't yet own it, reflect back on your values. What is missing? What will truly represent who you are and your values? What will reflect your true skills? Tweak it until you feel comfortable that your skills, values, and capabilities are accurately and compellingly presented.

Choose Applicable Skills

When I was an entertainment lawyer leading the production risk department at Viacom and I wanted to transition to a human resources business partner position, I spent weeks looking at similar roles online. I noticed that some of them were more tactically oriented while others seemed more strategic. Some mentioned "coaching" while others emphasized employee relations. Some were full-service HR business partner roles covering organizational design, talent management, career development, workforce planning, and performance reviews while others were narrower with just a few of those areas. I also looked up my HR business partner friends on LinkedIn to see what they wrote on their pages. As I narrowed down the areas I had experience in and the ones I would need experience in, I knew I had to use some key words to attract a recruiter and hiring a manager. This is where I landed (key words in **bold**):

> **STRATEGIC LEADER** with a track record of **solving complex organizational challenges** through **people-related solutions** that enhance **organizational effectiveness** and efficiencies, manage competing interests, and **build relationships** while bridging differences, resulting in **increased performance** and sustained **cross-organizational impact.**

Notice that my summary statement didn't mention "HR business partner" because I wasn't one. But I used key words that to me were all true. I used some of those capabilities cross-functionally and some just within our team and I created those outcomes. In looking at my experience through the lens of an HR role, I was able to show how my skills were directly applicable to the core concepts of HR.

Once you write that first sentence, the rest of your resume will flow. That sentence is your brand. It is who you are *today*. The rest of your resume should reflect the career you have chosen, not the jobs you left.

Chapter 8 Summary

1. **Set a theme:** Create a dynamic introductory statement with the first sentence that explains who you are and what skills you have that make you a solid candidate for the role.

2. **Dissect job descriptions:** Look for hard and soft skills to incorporate, and refine your introductory statement.

3. **Title yourself:** Determine the first few words that will label yourself in the strongest way and set the perception of how you will succeed in the job.

4. **Choose applicable skills:** Look at your current skills and responsibilities through the lens of the new role and pick out the most applicable to round out your first statement.

9

Highlighting Transferable Skills

"People with highly transferable skills may be specialists in certain areas, but they're also incredible generalists—something businesses that want to grow need."

—Leah Busque, Taskrabbit founder

The Experience section on your resume and LinkedIn profile is what attracts recruiters. Most resumes include a laundry list of everything a person has ever done, but that's not how to create an Experience section that stands out and attracts recruiters' interest beyond seven seconds. Experience is the most strategic section of a resume and should be used to showcase only those skills that are directly applicable to the prospective job. You may think that since you worked on an incredible project with a phenomenal outcome, it must be on your resume. But if that project isn't directly applicable to the job you are applying for and you can't find a way to make a case for it, it shouldn't be on your resume. Yes, I am asking you to leave off some of your greatest accomplishments in your life because they will only muddle your resume and confuse a recruiter if they aren't directly relevant to the roles you are pursuing. This is hard advice for most people to follow because it begs the question: What DO I put on my resume?

Tip #9: Your resume should only contain information that is directly applicable to your new career.

Aligning Experience with Skills

In the same way you made your introductory statement relate to the position you seek, determine how to make your experience relate to it. Print out (or copy/paste into a document) the job description and look at the needed skills, then shape your experience to align with those skills even if you don't have specific experience with that particular job.

1. Review "experience needed." The best place to research this is through job descriptions and on the LinkedIn profiles of those who are already working in your chosen career. Let's use an entry-level marketing coordinator position for our example. From looking at numerous such roles throughout the country, you can compile critical job requirements, highlighting the most important skills (**bold** for hard skills, underline for soft skills, and *italics* for information to use in a cover letter):

- Contribute to team **brainstorming sessions on creative and innovative marketing plans** which generate demand from our target audience.
- Coordinate details for **marketing campaigns** and **content development plans** including **budgets, deadlines, and creative deliverables,** ensuring all campaign needs are delivered in a timely fashion.
- Oversee **marketing request process** for **creative production, creating and updating project timelines, managing creative production, and coordinating deliverables.**
- Assist in the **creation of deliverables (presentations, handouts, images)** and **manage compliance approval process.**
- Act as **point person for creative development, managing workflow,** adjusting schedules based on priorities, maintaining on-going communication with key stakeholders and teams.
- **Coordinate production and distribution** of outreach materials such as brochures, handouts, signs, and giveaway items.
- **Monitor and analyze** the **performance of marketing efforts** including **developing reports**, and making recommendations to optimize efforts.

2. Match your skills. Now match your experience to the job description requirements as closely as possible using the STAR method: Situation, Task, Action, Result. "Situation" is the work being done or the challenge or issue that needs to be solved. "Task" describes the goal or what you want to achieve. "Action" is the work you do to bring about the solution and reach the goal. "Results" are the outcomes and measurement of those outcomes. The object is to incorporate as many pieces of STAR as you can into each bullet point of experience.

Look at all your internship, volunteer, and school experiences through the lens of the new career. This is why you need to write out your resume accomplishments before using AI. AI doesn't know what you have done and won't be able to translate your specific experiences through the lens of the new job. What key words from specific job descriptions and LinkedIn profiles of people who work in your field of choice relate to your previous work and experience? The following example, from a client trying to break into marketing, showcases some bullet points from internship experience (through the lens of a marketing coordinator) by using key words directly from job descriptions (**bold** for hard skills, <u>underline</u> for soft skills):

▸ <u>Collaborated</u> with brand marketing team on the **creation and delivery of proposals, calendars, project plans, timelines, creative deliverables, and strategic creative briefs.**

▸ Provided creative notes on **presentations, handouts, images,** and other **deliverables** in a timely manner.

▸ <u>Organized</u> **production and distribution of creative deliverables** to all stakeholders and managed approval **workflows.**

▸ <u>Actively contributed</u> to **content brainstorming sessions** and proactive pitches for earned media opportunities for clients in CPG and entertainment verticals resulting in a $3M business.

▸ Tracked and **analyzed** marketing campaign **performance** and **provided recommendations to optimize future campaigns.**

The "experience" on page 111 shows that this entry-level employee understands the lingo of marketing and has some experience with the basic job duties. And, again, her experiences don't lie. For example, while she hasn't overseen the marketing request process for creative production, she has project management experience and has worked side-by-side with leaders in this capacity. Connecting her experience to the skills and capabilities needed will show that she can be successful in the role. Finally, note that every bullet point doesn't conform to the STAR method, and they don't need to. If you *can* point to results, add them as often as possible.

If this entry-level employee did not have any marketing experience and didn't major in marketing, she could choose to take the next six months or so to gain that experience through courses, internships, and/ or shadowing someone in marketing to become more knowledgeable about what makes marketers successful in the workplace. She will make that determination from reviewing the necessary skills in job descriptions.

Here's another example. A graduating college senior worked at a national brand clothing store to put himself through college and didn't have the luxury of taking internships like his peers. He graduated with a degree in human resources and wants to move into that field, specifically in operations. His current resume includes his work at the clothing store:

> ▸ Maintained store appearance by organizing merchandise displays, replenishing stock, and ensuring cleanliness.
> ▸ Operated cash register and processed transactions accurately and efficiently.
> ▸ Collaborated with team members to achieve sales targets and contribute to a positive work environment.
> ▸ Handled inventory management tasks such as receiving shipments, conducting stock checks, and restocking shelves.
> ▸ Demonstrated flexibility by performing various duties as needed, including opening/closing procedures and assisting with store maintenance tasks.

However, HR operations job descriptions list *these* types of skills and experience: project management, onboarding (facilitating completion of required paperwork, orientation, training), technology implementation, customer service, customer satisfaction, creating and monitoring policies and procedures related to employee conduct, coordinating recruiting and hiring processes, workplace safety, compliance with state and federal regulations, analyzing employee productivity metrics and data. Further, some roles may prefer the PHR (Professional Human Resources certification) or the CAPM® (Certified Associate in Project Management). Looking at his store sales associate work through an HR operations lens, he can transform his resume by focusing only on accomplishments that are directly applicable to HR (see **bold** for keywords):

▶ **Customer Service**: Implemented **customer service** strategies, enhancing the **customer experience** which increased **customer satisfaction** metrics by 18%.

▶ **Onboarding Processes: Facilitated onboarding processes of new hires, including verifying completion of paperwork, conducting orientation sessions, and training on company policies, customer interaction, and product knowledge** to ensure **employee success** and continued **employee engagement and retention.**

▶ **Policies and Procedures:** Collaborated with senior leadership to implement and monitor **policies and procedures** related to **employee conduct, workplace safety, and compliance** with **state and federal** labor regulations.

▶ **Performance Management:** Implemented performance system including creating **employee productivity** assessment which identified and recognized top performers.

▶ **Recruitment:** Conducted **recruitment and selection processes** including **posting jobs, screening resumes, scheduling interviews, and making hiring recommendations.**

The previous example shows that, as a store sales associate, he understands HR concepts. He didn't qualify to take the PHR exam, but he was able to qualify to take the CAPM, showing his knowledge of best practices in project management which is valuable for any entry-level job in HR. A hiring manager would be able to see how his work ethic from his commitment to his job for four years while in school, along with his HR knowledge and experience could be a huge asset in an entry-level role, especially in the retail industry. Note: Nowhere on his resume does it say he works in HR, but refocusing his resume through the lens of HR shows he is performing specific HR-type functions while working as a store sales associate. Even though he had tremendous success in sales in his current job, sales accomplishments are not directly relevant to HR. For those achievements, clink glasses of champagne with a friend while leaving them off your resume, or they will become noise that distracts a recruiter from seeing your true value in the prospective job.

Chapter 9 Summary

1. **Review job descriptions:** Determine what experience is needed to be successful in the new career/job.

2. **Match experience:** Only add experiences to your resume that match the requirements and key words in the job description, preferably using the STAR method.

CHAPTER

Mind the Gap

"Life is a matter of choices, and every choice you make, makes you."
—John C. Maxwell, leadership author

Taking time off to travel the world after graduation. Taking time off in the middle of school to figure out what you want to do. Taking forced time off because the job market hampered your job search. Taking time off to simply . . . breathe. It doesn't matter why someone takes time off or has a non-working gap between school and finding that first job. Yet, this gap brings a tremendous amount of anxiety and fear to those looking for that first opportunity.

The most important thing to do on a resume regarding a gap is to own it: you made a choice (or the choice was made for you) to take time off. Then determine how to best position it on your resume or whether it needs to be positioned at all. If you choose to leave a time gap unfilled in your resume and it isn't easy to decipher why it's there, the recruiter and hiring manager will automatically speculate as to

Tip #10: Own the Gap

what the gap could be. The only way to prevent a recruiter from creating a false narrative or interpretation is to explain what happened clearly and succinctly on your resume since cover letters are rarely read.

Your resume is about marketing yourself in the best positive light, so the object is to find a way to show how that time off enhanced your qualifications for the job. By including the gap in your resume in a positive way, you will leave no room for inaccurate speculation. Think of it as a branding challenge: position that time off just as you would every other job you've had to make it relevant to the role you are applying to. Here are some common reasons why people take time off after school or during school and examples of how to position it on your resume.

Caring for a Sick Family Member or Yourself

This is noble and necessary, and if an employer faults you for this gap in your resume, that's not a company you want to work for anyway. Never say you were "stuck" caretaking. Own that you felt this was the most important job you could have in that moment and you were able to expand on your soft skills.

Caretaker

Self-Employed (or Independent), City 2023–2024

- ▸ Effectively communicated with healthcare providers and coordinated meetings with healthcare professionals, financial institutions, and legal firms while caring for a sick family member, giving her peace of mind.

- ▸ Acted as executor of estate and worked successfully with multiple creditors, including credit card companies, utilities, medical facilities, and banking institutions to close out all financials quickly and efficiently.

Someone applying for a finance job could discuss helping to manage the trust or other financial affairs. Pick the areas in caregiving that are most relevant to the role you are applying to. The first bullet point talks about effective soft skills such as communicating and multitasking. The second bullet point talks about the same soft skills but also shows financial acumen.

Two bullet points are enough; keep it simple. Notice that the description doesn't say "caring for a sick grandmother in hospice." That's too much detail. Also, never write "Leave of Absence." Those are legal and HR trigger words that aren't always looked upon favorably. The object is to give enough information to fill the gap without too much detail to make it personal or awkward.

Traveling the World

All I can say is, bravo! How many people take the time to see the world? The experience most certainly taught you global mobility but also about different cultures. In today's global workforce, understanding other cultures is critical. Recruiters also say a person who has taken a sabbatical after graduation and traveled is ready to find that perfect fit when they start looking for a new role. You will likely find more jealousy that you took the time in the first place than roadblocks to entry in the job market. Here is an example of how to position travel as both interesting and valuable if applying for global mobility jobs or any kind of coordinator role.

World Traveler   1/2024–8/2024

Independent or Self-Employed, *worldwide (or region such as EMEA or APAC if you traveled regionally)*

▸ Traveled to 10 countries in APAC to understand how cultural diversity in the workplace impacts decision-making in business.

▸ Managed all travel visas and work documents and maintained immigration compliance records for smooth entry into every country.

▸ Gained written understanding and verbal fluency in Mandarin and Japanese.

If you traveled the world and worked odd jobs, you could use the above example or change the job title to Entrepreneur and add a bullet point that is relevant to the job you are applying to—in this case, software engineering (in **bold**):

Entrepreneur   1/2024–8/2024

Various Companies, *India, Malaysia*

- ▸ Traveled to 10 countries in APAC to understand how cultural diversity in the workplace impacts decision-making in business.
- ▸ **Worked in various roles including consulting on software-based start-ups, providing tours, and teaching written and verbal English communication skills.**
- ▸ Gained written understanding and verbal fluency in Mandarin and Japanese.
- ▸ Managed all travel visas and work documents and maintained documentation and compliance records for smooth entry into every country.

If you took time off during school and it took you more than four years to graduate, you can merely put the graduation date on your resume and not the start date. It is up to you if you want to discuss that gap with a recruiter because it won't be obvious from your resume.

The most important thing to know is don't lie on your resume. While most companies will fire you if they find out you lied on your resume, there are extreme cases of people going to jail. It was widely reported that Veronica Hilda Theriault was convicted of deception, dishonesty, and abuse of a public office when she fabricated her employment experience and education to obtain a chief information officer role with South Australia's Department of the Premier and Cabinet.[1] She was sentenced to 25 months in jail!

While that seems extreme, it is, at the very least, unethical to lie on your resume about where you worked, where you went to school, and what you've accomplished in your career. Some people who lied on their resume have ruined their careers. In 2006, David Edmondson was forced to resign as CEO of Radio Shack[2] after the company discovered he had no college degree, though his resume showed he had two of them. Wayne Simmons was fired from being a Fox News commentator and "terrorism analyst" and then was immediately arrested after claiming to be a former CIA agent, which had helped him obtain government security clearances.[3] He was sentenced to 33 months in prison after he pled guilty to major fraud against the US, wire fraud, and a felony for illegally possessing a firearm.

Scare you enough? Good. Don't lie. That said, it's not unethical to position your accomplishments in a way to make them directly relevant to the role you are applying for.

Chapter 10 Summary

1. **Own the gap:** Make sure you address time gaps in your resume whether you were caring for a sick relative or traveling the world.

2. **Hone the narrative:** Determine your perspective on the gap and be able to confidently explain the reason in one or two sentences. Don't let the recruiter create the narrative.

3. **Don't lie:** Understand the difference between your "perspective" and a lie. Never lie about your experience or fill the gap with work you didn't do.

CHAPTER

Tell a Great Story in Your Cover Letter

"Storytelling is the calculated release of information."
—Alex Garland, English writer and filmmaker

When is the last time someone told you a great story about a friend and you sat there riveted, wanting to know more and more about that person? You asked questions and were insatiably curious about every detail of how they either overcame a horrific experience or celebrated a great triumph. This is what your cover letter should be designed to do—connect the dots to make recruiters and hiring mangers curious about you.

First, let's be real. Recruiters rarely read cover letters and hiring managers rarely even see them. They are sometimes separated from the resume in ATSs, and most hiring managers don't even know where to find them. Further, many tech companies don't even have a place to type or upload one. But if there is a place to upload or type a cover letter, should you do so? It depends.

Tip #11: Cover letters are meant to tell a great story.

Don't write one if . . .

→ your resume and LinkedIn profile are complete, you are fully qualified for the job, and you are applying for the exact job that matches your skill set.

→ you aren't a good writer and have no one to help you. The cover letter could be your first impression, and a badly written one— especially with grammatical errors—could make recruiters not want to screen you. (That said, you could use AI to help you, which I talk about more later.)

Do write one if . . .

→ the ATS or company requires a cover letter to submit the whole application.

→ your resume has gaps that you were unable to fill on your resume or your resume doesn't tell the whole story about you.

→ you are applying to a company that is collecting resumes via email or other non-ATS channels.

Your cover letter can also be used as your introductory email to a recruiter if you are reaching out directly. Further, since you won't know if an application requires a cover letter until you start applying online, it's a good idea to have one ready.

What Is Your Story?

While there are no strict rules for writing cover letters, this chapter will cover some of the basics. Simple cover letters should be three to four paragraphs at most, with two to three sentences in each paragraph.

Paragraph 1: Start with a catchy first line that isn't too "cutesy," then mention the job you are applying for and the skills you have that will make you a great fit for this position.

Sentence 1: Catch your reader with your first words. If you want someone to read your cover letter (assuming they even open it), your first few words should entice them to want to learn more about you.

The best example is when someone refers you, because referrals will always get you in the door faster than a random application. First line examples:

Someone referred you:

Product Manager John Smith referred me to the [name of role] because he believes I would be a great addition to [company name].

Analyst:

> If you were to analyze me, you would need to gather facts, so let me give you the basics about who I am and why I'm perfect for [company name] the business analyst position.

Human Resources:

> Listen. That is the number one thing I will do to build relationships and provide exceptional customer service in Human Resources Operations at [company name].

If you're worried about coming up with something unique that doesn't sound silly, approach the first line in a more traditional way:

Traditional:

> It is with great enthusiasm that I submit my application to [name of role] at [company name].

or

> Please accept my application for the [name of role] at [company name].

Sentence 2: State what role you are applying to and some information about you that makes you a great fit. "A, B, and C" in the examples below represent three things from the job description that match your experience.

Example:

> My experience in [A, B, and C] makes me a strong candidate for [company name/position].

Another way to go is to rely on your resume and introduce your cover letter as having something new:

> My experience, knowledge, and skills are outlined on my resume and LinkedIn profile, so I will take this opportunity to explain how I can bring unique value that would make me a perfect fit for [company name].

Paragraph 2: Use industry lingo and set your story. What experiences in your life or on your resume make you more unique or more qualified than any other entry-level candidate? Look at the job description and determine how your experience allows you to bring a distinct perspective to the role and company compared to other candidates. For example (**bold** for job description words):

> Experience gained from owning my own **digital marketing** business since I was ten years old will allow me to bring a unique perspective to your **digital marketing organization** because I understand the **customer journey** of **Gen Z** and [name of company] is seeking to **attract more Gen Z customers.**

This one sentence tells so much about this candidate: they are a go-getter and entrepreneurial but also understand the marketing lingo of "customer journey." They have researched and read media and press about the company's trajectory and mission to attract more Gen Z customers. This candidate's experience directly relates to the company's goals.

Another way to translate skills in a cover letter is to focus on soft skills with specific words from the job descriptions. This example could work for nearly any career:

> Remember when you were a kid and couldn't wait for your birthday to open all those presents? Every problem that needs a solution is like a present to me. My innate curiosity is endless, and that is what makes me unique among my peers. I have always been the one to ask the right question that helps the team come up with innovative solutions.

Paragraph 3 (optional): Back up paragraph 2 with a relevant and short three-to-four sentence story that explains the exact work you are doing in the capacity of the new role you are applying for.

> When interning at [company name], I helped farmers in Nebraska transition from traditional methods of monitoring crops and detecting pests to a more efficient solution of monitoring crop health, which minimized crop losses and optimized yields. I worked

with a team that was designing an autonomous agriculture drone equipped with advanced sensors and imaging technology to monitor crop health and detect pests in real time. I researched relevant technologies, designed a drone system with autonomous navigation and multispectral imaging, built a prototype of the drone hardware and software components, and piloted a monitoring system in a study on selected farms which gathered feedback from stakeholders and farmers to evaluate the effectiveness and usability of the system. I documented the design process, implementation details, and evaluation results in a comprehensive report with recommendations for future enhancements. Farmers are now using the drone system throughout the state.

The above shows that the writer has both hardware and software experience and understands the overall product development process, including hard skills such as algorithms and product design and soft skills such as stakeholder feedback.

Another option would be a project you worked on in college or even for a family business which had a big impact and is relevant to the job for which you are applying. Here's a good example from a client:

When a local artisanal bakery was facing challenges in expanding its customer base and increasing sales due to limited online visibility, I helped it develop a comprehensive digital marketing strategy to enhance the bakery's online presence, increase brand awareness, and improve customer engagement. Through conducting market research, analyzing competitors' digital marketing strategies, and identifing strengths, weaknesses, and areas for opportunity, I understood how to optimize the bakery's website for usability, performance, and SEO effectiveness and implemented improvements such as responsive design, faster loading times, and added new content with relevant key words. The implementation of the strategy grew website traffic by 50% in three months and increased online orders and reservations by 30% through additional email marketing campaigns and promotional offers.

The writer focuses on her digital marketing experience, showing she understands how to identify the problems to solve, the channels to employ to solve those problems, and how to track and measure the results. While there is a chance the above information could be condensed into a bullet point on a resume, it won't be nearly as effective as a story that shows influence, capability, and impact.

Paragraph 4: The close. (If you choose not to put in an example, then this is paragraph 3). The finish should be simple, no more than two sentences, emphasizing your desire to discuss your qualifications further:

> I hope I have persuaded you to see how my skills would make me a valuable asset in this exciting role at [company name]. I welcome the opportunity to meet with you about the position.

or

> I hope you can see my skills and experience are directly applicable to the [name of position.] I welcome the opportunity to meet with you to discuss further how I could bring value to [name of company]

Putting it all together. Here is the actual cover letter I used when I applied to Roku for the director, HR business partner role—my first job in HR. You'll notice, I took the more traditional approach (**bold** for job description key words):

> With a stellar record of **people management and development, identifying critical business needs, and implementing new approaches and programs to improve operational effectiveness in alignment with business strategy,** it is with excitement that I submit my resume for your consideration for Roku's Director, Human Resources G&A role. My diverse experience as a **strategic business leader** in a **decentralized and matrixed global media organization** makes me a standout candidate for this position.
>
> My rich experience, knowledge, and strengths are outlined on my resume and LinkedIn profile, so I will take this opportunity to explain how my skills directly translate to this position and why I am the

perfect fit for Roku. I have spent more than 15 years in **media and entertainment** providing **strategic guidance to employees,** from assistants to division presidents, in areas including **organizational effectiveness, talent growth, learning and development, and change management.** I not only understand, but my track record shows, **excellence in implementing modern HR principles to engage employees, starting with recruiting, and continuing through employees' growth with the company.**

To highlight one success story: as one of my employees was finishing her MBA with a concentration in data science, it was clear she had **gained skills** that could be valuable to the company but could not be fully utilized in my department. While I provided her some analytics projects, she clearly wanted to **stretch her skill set** into a more technical area. As sad as it was to lose such a stellar employee in my department, I championed her move into the Data Science department where her **skills could best benefit the company.**

My passion for people and how they **contribute to business success,** combined with my **global reach, business acumen, and emotional intelligence in coaching,** makes me a stellar candidate for your Director, Human Resources role. I hope I have persuaded you to understand how my skills would make me a valuable asset in this role.

I welcome the opportunity to meet with you about the position.

Best,
Marlo Lyons

In the above example, you see the positioning is about employee retention and aligning people skills with company goals. And, the cover letter told a story, positioning all my skills through the perspective of the new job.

Notice, though, that I never said in my cover letter, "While I haven't worked in HR . . ." There is no reason to disclose where your experience comes from in an organization. It is about skills and capabilities, not hierarchy.

I wrote the recruiter a message through LinkedIn after I applied online:

Hi Bob,

I'm reaching out to you to directly express my excitement about the Director, Human Resources G&A role at Roku, Inc. My extensive experience in entertainment combined with my legal history and specific strategic experience would make me a tremendous asset to Roku in this role. I hope you will seriously consider me for this position and give me an opportunity to explain further how I can bring outside-the-box value to the company.

Thank you!
Marlo

He responded and we set up time to talk on the phone. While Bob told me he didn't read the cover letter until after we chatted for the first time, he did leverage some of the information to convince the hiring manager, the head of HR, to talk to me.

Another way to approach a cover letter is to cover your soft skills while explaining your experience. The trick is to not repeat your resume. Here is an example (**bold** for key words):

I am writing to express my interest in the **financial analyst position** at [company name]. My passion for leveraging my **finance** experience and knowledge combined with my soft skills would allow me to bring great value to [company name.].

Throughout my academic and internship experiences, I have cultivated a **strong foundation in finance** while honing essential soft skills that are critical for success in the **financial industry.** My internships not only helped me gain **proficiency in financial analysis, forecasting, and risk management,** but also in **stakeholder alignment, influence, communication and simplifying complex information.**

One of my key strengths is my ability to **effectively align stakeholders toward common goals.** During my internship at [company name], I analyzed **large datasets and synthesized findings into actionable insights** for **senior management.** By breaking down **complex financial data and presenting it in a user-friendly format,** I empowered leadership to make **informed decisions** with confidence.

I am enthusiastic about the opportunity to discuss how my skills and experiences can bring value to your team.

Best,

[your name]

Use of AI

While AI can be useful in helping you organize your thoughts, it shouldn't be used to write your cover letter from scratch. AI doesn't know your greatest accomplishments or your story like you do. It also will give you a generic cover letter which will not impress recruiters. I suggest if you need help writing a cover letter, write yours first, then ask an AI program such as ChatGPT to rewrite it or make it more dynamic. But read the results carefully! You wouldn't want AI to say you did something you have no idea how to do!

Final Tips

A couple final tips of what not to write in cover letters:

1. **"I."** Don't start every sentence with "I." Find other ways such as with "My."

2. **Don't copy/paste.** Cover letters are not meant to reiterate your resume; that's why you have a resume. Cover letters are meant to enhance what's on your resume with soft skill descriptions and how your skills will transfer easily to the current role.

3. **Research for tone.** How do you know whether to go with a fun or traditional route in your cover letter if you haven't worked at the company? Research. Look for how the company describes its culture. Easygoing? Fast-paced? Is the company

big or small? You will also pick up clues from the way a company describes itself in its various communications and "About Us" documents.

4. **Don't get personal.** Don't talk about your kids or husband, wife, girlfriend, boyfriend, significant other, etc.

5. **It's not about you.** Don't talk about what the role will teach you or what you hope to learn. Cover letters are about *the value you bring to the company.*

6. **Proper grammar/punctuation.** The same advice for resumes goes for cover letters. Write using complete sentences with proper grammar. If you don't know how to use a semicolon, learn before using one. If you aren't a good writer, have someone read it for you before sending it. This could be the first, second, or third impression a hiring manager has of you. If they like you after reviewing your resume and then read a poorly written cover letter, it will give that recruiter serious pause as to whether to keep advocating your candidacy.

Chapter 11 Summary

1. **What is your story?** Write down two or three stories that relate your current experience to the new job. Shorten the story to four sentences or less.

2. **Paragraph 1:** Introduce yourself with a catchy or a traditional opening that explains who you are, who referred you (if applicable), what role you are applying for, and how your skills are perfect for the role.

3. **Paragraph 2 (and 3 if needed):** Tell a good story that incorporates hard/soft skills that are directly relatable to the role based on the job description.

4. **Paragraph 4:** This is a closing statement requesting a chance to further explain the value you can bring to the company.

12

Leverage LinkedIn

(and other professional websites)

"Your LinkedIn profile should leave no room for doubt about the kind of job you're looking for and why you're the best person for that position."

—Melanie Pinola, *LinkedIn in 30 Minutes*

Back when I was applying for my first job, I had a Brother word processor, fancy stationery, fancy matching envelopes, and stamps. That was the only way to apply for jobs. Resumes were photocopied or printed onto nice paper and sent out one by one with cover letters. Then you would wait to hear something, anything. Today we have LinkedIn, Monster, Indeed, Glassdoor, Simply Hired etc. While each website has slightly different offerings and benefits, LinkedIn is the single most important asset for a job hunter as well as the single most important asset in networking. Quite frankly, LinkedIn is your greatest asset when it comes to finding a new job, transitioning to a new career, or meeting people in your industry or other industries. And it's the best way for people to find you.

At any given moment, approximately 30 million companies have pages on LinkedIn. That means 30 million companies regularly use LinkedIn to source people for employment. In fact, at any given moment, 20 million jobs and 90,000 schools are listed

> **Tip #12: Leverage LinkedIn (and other professional websites) to make it easy for recruiters to find you.**

on LinkedIn worldwide. There is no better place to find the job of your dreams than LinkedIn. And there is no better place for recruiters to find you than on LinkedIn. In fact, many recruiters have told me they are skeptical about an applicant's experience if they don't have a LinkedIn profile.

Once you have a LinkedIn profile, recruiters should be reaching out to you proactively without you even needing to apply for jobs. Recruiters say the number one way they find candidates is by doing a Boolean search with key words from the job description on LinkedIn. Therefore, if you aren't hearing from recruiters, it's because your profile either isn't as complete as it could be, or you haven't positioned yourself properly for the jobs/career you want to move into. So how do you get recruiters to find you? You leverage every field on LinkedIn.

Filling in LinkedIn Fields

1. Personal photo: The number one thing people look at on LinkedIn is your profile picture. In fact, LinkedIn reports profile pictures get twenty-one times more profile views than profiles without pictures. Your picture should be you, alone, from the shoulders up, dressed in professional clothes against a neutral, plain, and simple background setting. You aren't outside in the woods (unless you are a forest ranger or looking to be a bike tour guide) and you aren't standing in front of a distracting background. You don't wear a sorority formal dress or a wedding tux no matter how stunning you look because that's not for a work environment. Your picture is also not a fraternity or yearbook picture, which is a bit too professionally stiff. And it is not you in a group shot.

How do you get such a perfect picture? Most people have cell phones and know how to take a nice picture. Dress nice, put on makeup if applicable, do your hair, and stand in a neutral location but not too close to a wall where you will have a shadow. Consider having your hair or makeup professionally done at the mall or at a store like Sephora or any makeup counter in a department store like Macy's. That's how I was able to secure a professional photo.

I was invited to an event at the local mall that offered a "makeup makeover" and up to fifteen professional photos on a zip drive if I bought $75 worth of product. I needed some product anyway, so I thought, *Why not?* I had my hair professionally blow-dried before the event and gave clear instructions to the makeup artist to keep the makeup subtle for a professional headshot. At least six other women were doing the same! These types of events happen all the time. All you have to do (if you wear makeup) is check the makeup counters at stores like Bare Naked, Mac, or Sephora to see if a particular brand has any upcoming events or visit the brand's website.

Rule of thumb: Update your picture every five years or if your appearance has changed dramatically (e.g., you had long hair and now it is pixie short) or you lost or gained weight in your face. LinkedIn isn't a dating site, but your picture should look like you or an interviewer might question your integrity or self-esteem.

My last piece of advice is to smile or at least have an approachable expression. Smiling makes you look inviting and warm and suggests that you don't take yourself too seriously. It should make someone want to get to know you, even have lunch with you! In the interviewing section, I will explore how to convey that warmth in conversation.

2. Background photo. It's not critical to change the stock photo that's there, but if you have a background photo that is more inviting, add it. Be careful not to pick one that is too busy or distracting. Simple colors/ simple message is best. Further, make sure the photo works on mobile devices.

3. Headline. The headline under your name will be pulled from your most current job, but you can edit it. Pick a headline that conveys who you are and what experience you have as you define yourself in your new career. For example, an early career digital marketer may use, "Digital

Marketer | Social Media Strategist | SEO / PPC Campaign Manager | Content Amplifier." This is how this early career candidate wants to be seen and where they can bring value. Use this headline along with your transferable experiences to define yourself in your new career.

4. Summary. The "About" section on LinkedIn is one of the biggest missed opportunities to provide a short snippet of who you are. If you don't see this section, add it under "Add profile section - About." This is where you put the introductory statement that is at the top of your resume, so it's okay to copy/paste. If you are applying for various kinds of jobs, then use a more generic or a broader summary on your profile. After the introductory statement, consider adding your "Core Skills." Bullet-point each one and make sure there are key words from job descriptions in each as long as those key words are applicable to your experience. This section should not only reflect your experience but also your personality if you are able to showcase that.

5. Experience. LinkedIn states that profiles with completely filled-in experiences are ten times more likely to get messages and responses from recruiters. Experience on LinkedIn, if positioned properly with words from descriptions of the jobs you want, should attract recruiters through their searches. It is critical to be as clear on LinkedIn as you are on your resume, but LinkedIn is not meant to be your resume. It is meant to entice an employer with highlights about who you are and what you have accomplished.

I am asked all the time, "Should I copy my resume onto LinkedIn?" You can and that is fine. You can also shorten or elongate what you put on LinkedIn. If you choose to copy/paste from your resume, you will have bullet points on LinkedIn; otherwise, there is no bullet point option. Some people would rather put short paragraphs under the job title instead of bullet points. That is fine, too, if it's only two or three sentences with active verbs and includes an overview of your experience that includes key words from a summary of the job descriptions of the job you want. But keep in mind, most recruiters and hiring managers don't read long paragraphs. As you are updating your LinkedIn experience, make sure your overall LinkedIn experience timeline matches the timeline on your resume. If it doesn't match, recruiters will consider that a red flag.

6. Education: Education is meant to give a high-level overview of your accomplishments and where you went to school. It is not a place to list every award received or activity you participated in. Your most recent degree should be listed first. If you have an MBA and a bachelor's, the MBA goes first. You don't have to add the actual dates you entered and finished your education or your GPA unless you want to. What matters is that you achieved the degree. Further, most companies don't care about GPA. If you are going into venture/investment banking or finance, they do care! If you think the years will help you because the hiring manager went to the same school or you have a GPA of over 3.5, then feel free to include it.

If you have any specific activities from college that are relevant to the role, include them under "Education." For example, if you were the president of the school's marketing club and brought in big-name speakers, include a sentence on the knowledge/experience gained that shows you have some skills in marketing. For example:

President, Marketing Club
- Brought in chief marketing officers from [company names] to educate the membership about different marketing practices such as brand, product, communications, public relations, and marketing operations and the difference between working at an agency versus working in-house at a company.

If you are the first one in your family to graduate college or graduated at the top of your class while working full time, list that. It will make for a good talking point. Here is how mine looked when I was still looking for a corporate job and I had been out of school more than ten years:

Oklahoma City University School of Law

JD, Rank #2 / Magna Cum Laude   1999–2002

Activities and Societies: *Law Review*, Phi Delta Phi Legal Honor Society, writer for *The Verdict*

Attended OKCU night law school while working full time as a television news reporter and graduated in 3 1/2 years; ranked #2. (I just couldn't beat that guy Paul—he was SMART! Thank goodness I was smart enough to make him my study partner.)

- Published Note: "Switching Stations: The Battle over Non-compete Agreements in the Broadcasting Industry." 2002
- Covered US Supreme Court hearing for KWTV / Published Comment: "Earls ex rel. Earls v. Board of Education: Violating the Fourth Amendment's Spirit"

The George Washington University

BA, Political Communication

A few explanations about the above: I did add the year of my graduation from law school but not from undergrad. Why? I earned my undergrad degree in the '90s with a 3.4 GPA. That's a long time ago and makes me "old" in some employers' minds. And while I was proud of my GPA, a 3.4 doesn't mean much decades later. For law school, I wanted to show that I have had a legal mind since 2002. For those employers who like to do math and think I went to law school right after graduating college, they will believe I am eight years younger than I am. Their fault, not mine. (Shame on them for trying to do the math!)

As a new graduate you will want to at least put your graduation date so the recruiter knows when you are available to start a new job. You can put "Anticipated May [year]" or just "May [year]."

And while no one really cares what I did twenty-five-plus years ago, the *Law Review* and legal honor society convey that I am smart, while *The Verdict* shows I am a writer. Former lawyers who may now be hiring managers know that being published is a great achievement. I have since removed all of this detail, as it is no longer relevant to my current career trajectory. Remember when I said there is no right or wrong? If it feels right or conveys an important message about who you are, put it in, such as running ten marathons, being a collegiate athlete, or climbing Mount Kilimanjaro because these all show grit and determination.

In my case, notice the two sentences that humorously describe the overlap between school and work. In this case, in stating I went to law school at night while working full-time, I was trying to convey my ability to successfully multitask. That is not just a skill in and of itself but will resonate with a lot of hiring managers who have conquered night or weekend college or graduate school while working full time. It's also part of my "story" when I talk about my transition from TV news to working in entertainment. As for Paul, I should thank him because he not only taught me a lot when we were in school, but he has become quite the talking point with recruiters and gave me an opportunity to show my personality a bit. Thanks, Paul!

7. Licenses and certifications: Make sure you include all of these, especially if the license or certification is relevant to the role. While I no longer practice law daily, it does have relevance and that's why I keep my license active. Put all such achievements in order of relevance. My coaching certifications and SPHR and GPHR are listed above the law license.

8. Volunteer experience: Include it here, not on your resume unless your volunteer experience is the only directly relevant experience you have to your chosen career. It makes you human and tells a little more about you as a person than what your work history reveals. Write a short paragraph (two or three sentences) about what you did, what the organization does, and the impact that volunteering had on you and/or the people you were helping. "I" is fine to use in this section as long as most of the messaging is about the organization. If you use volunteer experience in the experience section, then don't use "I."

9. Skills and endorsements: Endorsements of your skills can be powerful. If you have some of the relevant skills for a new career, add them to your Skills section and click the applicable boxes to have them show up under each applicable job/internship. Further, your manager or colleagues can endorse you in these skills. For example, I was coaching a lot in my previous job even though it wasn't in my previous career's job description. After I added coaching to my skills list, I asked anyone who had experienced my coaching to please endorse me. LinkedIn also allows you to pin the top three to be seen at a glance on your profile. When recruiters do a Boolean search, these skills could help you be found. Since most recruiters won't open the tab to see all your skills, make sure the top three are directly relevant to the career you are seeking. Don't ignore this section. Skills endorsements can draw attention and should be optimized.

10. Recommendations: This section is critical. How do you get recommendations? If you have interned, volunteered, or worked, ask your former manager or a coworker to write you a recommendation. If you don't know people in your chosen career, then it's impossible to get a reference from them, which means you'll have to tap into your network to get some recommendations. I also recommend sending the people who agree to write a recommendation for you a few topics or bullet points of what you'd like them to cover. Otherwise, they could all sound the same. For example:

> Hi Jon,
>
> Thank you so much for agreeing to write a recommendation for me on LinkedIn. As you know, I'm applying for roles in the marketing field. I'd appreciate it if you would cover my ability to work in a chaotic, fast-paced environment and my ability to adapt to change. Also, if you can write a bit about the work I did at the company on [name of] product launch or the impact I made, that would be ideal.
>
> Thank you again,
> [your name]

Whether the recommendation is from your current internship, job, or volunteer activity or a previous one, always make sure the reference knows to relate your current work to the job you want. For example,

Brenda Madden is a colleague from my reporting days, and I asked her to write me a recommendation when I was transitioning to an HR role. TV news reporting and HR have very few similarities, so I asked her to write a recommendation that covered my professional presence, communication and interpersonal skills, work ethic, and ability to multitask under extreme pressure and deadlines. She wrote the following:

> Marlo and I worked together as reporters in Dayton, Ohio.
> Since then, I have watched her become a rising star in the corporate world. Her exceptional interpersonal and communication skills, combined with a professional presence developed from years of on-air reporting, have always allowed her to stand out among her colleagues. As a reporter, your job is to convince people to talk to you on camera during the most stressful times of their lives. It also requires you to find creative solutions to meet the needs of multiple people—producers, editors, photographers, the news director, and, of course, the viewer. Marlo's unique ability to do that often led to coveted assignments, including overseas travel to Israel and numerous high-profile stories. Those skills also prepared Marlo for her success today.
>
> As an attorney, she manages multiple priorities simultaneously and possesses a work ethic that would rival even the most accomplished CEO. But the quality that makes her a true asset is her ability to care. As a journalist, she cared about every person she met and every story she told. As a co-worker, she cared about the success and well-being of her colleagues. Her drive to excel made her a leader in our newsroom, the type of employee who motivates everyone to do their best, so it's not surprising that she continues to be a driving force to this day.

This is the strongest recommendation in that section because she wrote about me as a human being within the context of my work. This allows people to know me better without having to talk to me. Having someone write about your soft skills is even more important than your hard skills, especially as you mature in your career. If your colleagues aren't good writers, write your own recommendation as an example or send bullet points and ask them to edit it in their voice based on what they want to say.

11. Follow industry organizations and groups. Are you following industry groups so you will see articles by them? Look for state, regional, and national industry groups that are relevant to the career you want to move into. Follow companies that you want to work for or that interest you. You will see articles by these groups that may help with lingo, contacts, and understanding the new career. Following industry groups also shows you are serious about the new career.

What *Not* to Put on your LinkedIn Profile

- → **Your grades.** Your school grades are irrelevant. Multiple headlines suggest many millionaires were not the best students.[1] Grades are not indicative of your success in the workplace.

- → **Your hobbies.** If you like to ski, great! Cook? Fantastic! Save it for Facebook, Instagram, or other social media platforms. LinkedIn is for professional posts only and your profile should exemplify that.

- → **"I" or "My."** Just like your resume, do not use "I" or "My" on your profile unless you are writing about your volunteering activities.

- → **Name-dropping just to name-drop.** Name-drop only if it matters. If you worked directly with Richard Branson on a project, or you interned for CAA and helped Jon Stewart solve a problem, then you can mention their names. The only reason you would name drop is to show you aren't intimidated by executives or stars. But only name-drop if there is obvious strategic value because the risk is it could turn off a recruiter or hiring manager.

➔ **Confidential or proprietary information.** LinkedIn is not a place to post anything that might be seen as confidential to the company you worked for. For example, many companies don't disclose their client lists or the projects they work on. Further, government employees have dozens of confidential projects and listing even the names of the projects could be an issue. If you only work on confidential projects, cover your employment history broadly with the skills used to be successful in that career instead of the names of projects or companies that benefited from your work.

Check Your LinkedIn Settings

Once your profile is as complete as it can be, make sure the "backend settings" are what you want. Click on your small picture/"Me" icon on the toolbar, review each of the settings, and decide which ones make the most sense. Two key settings are the following:

➔ Under "How others see your profile and network information," click on "Edit your public profile" and choose "Public" so you can be found.

➔ Under "Job Seeking Preferences," make sure you click on "Let recruiters know you're open to opportunities." If you want recruiters to find you, make it easy for recruiters to know by choosing the right settings.

Other Social Media

LinkedIn is not the only place to build a profile or to communicate your experience. You can post your resume for free on Monster.com, Indeed .com, CareerBuilder.com, ZipRecruiter, Glassdoor, Craigslist, TheMuse, and USAjobs.gov. Your local college may also have a job- or resume-posting site. Finally, associations or organizations are a great place to post your resume and make connections. There are hundreds of them, and some are specific. For example, the American Association of Blacks in Energy (AABE) was developed to provide thought leadership in the development of energy policies and regulations, emerging technologies, and environmental issues. On AABE's website, members who work in the energy industry can post resumes and search for jobs. Whatever field you are interested in, google the subject and association for an opportunity to not only post your resume but to network!

Chapter 12 Summary

1. **Leverage LinkedIn and other professional websites:** Use these powerful networking and candidate-searching tools to the fullest extent.

2. **Picture:** Take a head-and-shoulders picture in front of a solid background.

3. **Summary:** Include an introductory statement of who you are and any specific expertise or skills in the "About" section. Also add listed skills and competencies to this section.

4. **Experience:** Copy/paste your work history from your resume. Add more detail with key words as necessary.

5. **Education:** Include activities and publications if timely and relevant.

6. **Licenses and certifications:** List the most relevant ones first.

7. **Skills endorsements:** Ask former managers or colleagues to endorse the relevant skills needed for the new career.

8. **Volunteer activities:** Use this section to humanize your profile, showing your personality and the causes you are interested in.

9. **Recommendations:** Ask a minimum of three former managers or colleagues to write recommendations that describe your hard and soft skills and tie your current or past work to the career you are pursuing post college.

10. **Follow organizations:** Find at least five organizations that are relevant to the new career and follow them.

11. **Other social media:** Don't just rely on LinkedIn. While most recruiters will find you here, posting your resume on other career, association, or college websites will allow you to network and also be found by hiring managers who have similar interests.

13

Interviewing:
The Recruiter Screen

"I sometimes find that in interviews you learn more about yourself than the person learned about you."

—William Shatner, actor, author

YES! A recruiter reaches out to you via LinkedIn, email, or phone and would love to set a time to talk. Your response to that inquiry and your chat with the recruiter will create the very first personal impression beyond your resume and LinkedIn profile. Think about that—the very first personal impression. And yet, recruiters report that some candidates take that first phone call in the grocery store line, on a city street with sirens blaring, or while they are chewing gum or eating lunch (chomp, chomp). None of these locations or situations are okay! Candidates have also answered the phone with, "Yo, John here," or "Hello? Is this a scammer?" or simply "Hello." Then the recruiter identifies him/herself and the person says, "Who?" Recruiters can only think, "Seriously?" These screens should be taken more seriously than the hiring manager interview because you won't get to the hiring manager if you don't pass the recruiter screen.

> **Tip #13: The recruiter will determine whether you have the hard and soft skills to fit the role and the company during the initial screen.**

Respond to Every Recruiter Call

If the recruiter asks you for a time to chat, set a time where you will be in a quiet place with a good phone or internet signal. If you know you have a day full of back-to-back classes, don't "fit in" the call between classes. Find a day, time, and place to speak where you can compose yourself a half-hour before the scheduled call. Even if you have to wait a week before you get such an opening, the recruiter will likely still want to speak to you, but if other candidates are in play, there's a chance you may miss the window. Simply put, you won't be presented to a hiring manager if you *don't* make a good impression on the recruiter, so it's worth it to wait, if necessary.

Your timely response to an initial recruiter contact is just as important as subsequent calls because the recruiter will gauge your interest by how fast you first respond. If you are working full-time while applying for jobs, check your voicemail, LinkedIn messages, and personal email while on breaks or after work. (Even if you are not actively looking, keep your antenna out for potential opportunities.) Also, your email responses need to be clear and concise and free of grammatical errors. The recruiter is not your friend, so responding back with, "Hey, sounds great," or using abbreviations like this will raise a red flag: "I'd love to hear about the role, but I have an EMC tomorrow so I'm not available until Friday. IDK if you're available in the evening hours?" (That's "early morning class" and "I don't know" for those who aren't familiar.) Even if you would never work for the company the recruiter is contacting you about, set up the call and use the time to impress the recruiter with who you are. Remember, recruiters move and get hired to recruit for new roles and new companies every day. Also, you never know when an opportunity you never thought would interest you does pops up.

A close friend and colleague of mine, Samantha, had been working at a major entertainment company as a lawyer for five years. She loved her job and the people around her including her boss. It had all the flexibility she needed with two small children at home. She could walk to work and even go home to have lunch with her kids. She had no intention of leaving and thought she'd eventually take her boss's job when he retired. But one thing was missing: VP stripes. It wasn't about the title; it was about a title that was commensurate to her experience that would also set her up as his successor. Then LinkedIn sent her an ad for a coveted position at a leading tech company. She applied online and a company recruiter called her a few hours later! She thought maybe she'd use an offer as leverage to be promoted to VP in her current role, but the more she talked to the recruiter and hiring manager, the more intrigued she became. In addition to the same flexibility, she found more pay, better benefits, and a presumably great manager (she hoped!). By the end of the process, the tech company had won her over and she's still there today. That great manager worked out!

Research the Recruiter

Once you've scheduled a time to talk to a recruiter, prepare for the screening interview by researching the recruiter. Yes! Research the recruiter! Is it an internal or external recruiter? What types of candidates does the recruiter seek? Learn who the recruiter is and what they specialize in. Also check to see if you have any mutual connections on LinkedIn. If the recruiter asks about one of them, be prepared with an answer, such as how well you know "John" or that it's a random connection based on mutual respect for each other's career and experience in the field.

Research the Potential Job

If the recruiter told you the name of the company or the job title, find the job description that will be posted on the company's website and/ or on LinkedIn and research the company. Sometimes the recruiter will attach the job description to the initial email or give a link. It is your job to understand what industry the company is in, what companies are considered the competition to the company you are interviewing with and read any information on the company's goals and values.

What to Expect in the Recruiter Call

From researching the recruiter, company, and role, you can establish your strategy on what theme or message you want to leave with the recruiter and how your experience would be valuable to the company he or she is representing. The recruiter screen usually lasts between 20 and 30 minutes for entry level jobs and has four purposes:

1. Explain the role and company to you. The job description never covers every aspect of the job. Recruiters meet with hiring managers to discuss the intangibles, which are either described on the screening call or the recruiter will ask questions to detect if you have them. Intangibles can mean the hiring manager wants someone who went to a certain type of school or worked in certain type of internship. I remember one hiring manager saying he only wanted college athletes who had the relevant skills because they understand how to compete.

2. Make sure you have the hard skills. The job description is a wish list of hard and soft skills that the ideal candidate should possess. The recruiter will have discussed with the hiring manager which hard skills are absolute "musts," or foundational to the role, and which are not as important. Reminder, hard skills are the actual skills needed for the role such as sales-force proficiency, SQL expertise, or specific writing skills. Most of that is covered on your resume or LinkedIn profile, so the recruiter is just confirming that you have the experience you say you have (they may ask for examples) so they can check off those boxes.

3. Gauge your soft skills. As you answer questions about your hard skills, recruiters are gauging your soft skills. Some soft skills that relate to the workplace are cognitive flexibility, decision-making, influencing, learning quickly, working outside of structured processes, working cross-functionally, interpersonal skills, and being solution oriented. Remember the soft skills listed the Global Workplace Report in chapter 3? Refer back to that chapter because these are the most critical soft skills to have on your resume and understand how they play out in the workplace. As you answer questions about projects and accomplishments, make sure you describe how you influenced leaders in decision-making. Consider your tone while you are talking. Do you seem either arrogant or too humble as you describe your accomplishments? Do you talk in circles but never get to the point? Do you think you're having a nice debate but you are really being argumentative on an issue? How you discuss your qualifications matters.

For example, one person asked me, "Please describe the steps you took to introduce a big change to a group or company." Before I worked in HR and early in my interviewing process, I described how I rolled out a safety program at Viacom by working with outside counsel, drafting required documents, and presenting the program at roll-out meetings. One recruiter asked me, "Was the program easily adopted?" That's when I realized my story was leaving out the most important parts of the answer: the soft skills I used to accomplish the goal and what I learned from the adoption process. For example, I'd left out the stakeholder management piece—preflighting the information to get buy-in and influencing those who would be responsible for program compliance, which would be a lot more work. Showing you learned something from a project shows self-awareness, which is a key skill for any job. So, try to fit some soft skills into every answer about hard skills.

4. Determine whether you are a culture fit. The recruiter will listen to how you discuss your experience to assess whether you will be a culture fit within a company. Are you quiet? Loud? Too energetic? Enjoy working late? It may be okay to be all these things or none of them depending on the unique culture of the company. There is no point in putting you through the full interview process at a company if the recruiter knows the fit would be wrong.

Merriam-Webster describes culture as "the set of shared attitudes, values, goals, and practices that characterizes an institution or organization." A simpler description: "Culture is a way of being within a company."[1] For example, some cultures may require consensus before a decision is made, while others listen to all ideas but the decision-maker has unilateral authority even if the decision is the opposite of what the majority believes is right. If you are interviewing for a company where you could be overruled even though your idea is the best, the recruiter will probe if you can handle that or whether it will frustrate you. Or if you are applying to a start-up, you may be asked if you are comfortable with a lot of change, chaos, and loosely defined swim lanes on projects.

Netflix has an especially unique culture that it lays it out for candidates on its website.[2] It describes employees working on a "Dream Team" where everyone is extraordinary at what they do as well as highly effective collaborators. Low-performing employees are routinely terminated. The Netflix website essentially admits it: "Many people value job security very highly and would prefer to work at companies whose orientation is more about stability, seniority, and working around inconsistent employee effectiveness." That pretty much says, perform if you want to stay. Slackers should not apply. Roku had a similar cultural identity, calling it a "sports team" (not a "family," as some do). The line I heard most often was, "You don't pay your family to work with you and perform." A sports team requires that everyone bring consistent excellence or risk being kicked off the team (demoted to a lower league, cut, waived, contract not renewed). "Kicked off the team," in HR speak, means fired.

Amazon has a similar culture but also a specific way of holding meetings, where Jeff Bezos had reportedly banned PowerPoint presentations.[3] Instead, they've been replaced with a detailed six-page memo that must be read by everyone in the meeting before it can start. Even with Bezos no longer at the helm, Amazon believes that memos provide deeper clarity on an issue and create more effective communication. It can take a week or more to draft a memo and numerous people may edit it. Recruiters for Amazon thus screen applicants for their ability to embrace Amazon's mission and strategy as well as its unique communication style and a candidate's ability to draft a memo that fits the culture. Amazon's culture is so unique, there are dozens of blogs and even a course about how to prepare for an interview.[4]

Culture may also include how fast a company moves in making decisions, how much work each person is expected to accomplish, and whether employees are expected to answer emails after normal working hours or on weekends. At Roku, the pace was intense and incredibly fast.

Most people were emailing and working before they arrived at the office and long after they left in the evening. They would also text and email on weekends. I thrived in that fast-paced environment, but it also felt like a treadmill that at times I wanted to get off.

By comparison, the very first thing I noticed about the culture at Intuitive was that I rarely received emails at night or on weekends. I would check my phone over and over—even restart it to make sure the Outlook app was working—before I realized the culture didn't require nonstop communication. There was certainly a lot of work to do, but you were expected to spend uninterrupted quality time with your family when you were home. Moving to a role at Intuitive meant more time being 100% focused on my kids in off-work hours, not half-focused on them while trying to keep up with the needs of the business. It was a hard adjustment for me after working at such a frenzied pace for the previous decade.

While you can understand pieces of a company's culture by asking about it, there is no way to absorb all the nuances until you live it. I asked about culture during my Intuitive interview and was told that the people were really nice, the leaders were smart, and everyone believes in the company's mission. Every interviewer pointed to the leadership and individual expectations framed on the wall and said that employees truly live by those. It all sounded rewarding and purpose driven. Some of the leaders asked why I'd want to leave Roku, which had to be more exciting than "boring med-tech." They had alluded to the company's products being in a highly regulated industry but also emphasized how much work there was to do, so I didn't quite grasp how different work would be at the new company. I even called a few friends of friends who worked there, and from all the questions I asked, and information provided, I still didn't know I'd have mostly free nights and weekends. Adapting to this "quieter" job was a blessing and yet also a struggle. In fact, my boss said her biggest concern was my ability to adapt. She almost didn't hire me because culture is harder to teach than hard skills. Fortunately, I figured out how to still be "me" while adapting to a slower pace. Then the pace picked up and I realized it really wasn't that slow at all. That particular culture expected me to take time to learn first before jumping in, and I fully jumped into the crazy busy stage about a year into the job. But my nights and weekends still remained mostly free!

There is nothing worse for a recruiter or hiring manager than realizing that a new hire has the perfect experience and will drive business but that certain aspects of their personality or how they conduct business are antithetical to the company culture. Sometimes a new hire will realize that something is wrong but can't figure out what. At other times, they perform how they think they should and don't receive direct feedback of what isn't working which alienates co-workers or customers. It's not the "what" a new employee is doing but the "how." That is why recruiter screens are keenly focused on culture fit.

Prepare Answers to These Four Questions

Instead of seeing recruiters as gatekeepers, think of them as the experts who know whether you will be successful in a role. From that first phone call, the recruiter will know whether to sell you or not even mention you to the hiring manager for the next interview stage; your fate is in their hands. Being prepared for this screen and presenting yourself in the most favorable and accurate light is critical. How will they determine if you are a right fit? They will ask what seem like introductory or innocuous questions, but how you answer these four questions are key to whether you are a culture fit:

1. **"Tell me a little about yourself."** This question unnerves nearly everyone. Do you talk about your internship and volunteer history? Do you walk through your resume? How about your hobbies? What does a recruiter want to hear when asking you this question? Essentially, they want to get to know you. They want to get a feel for your energy, ability to communicate, whether you are super serious or can be personable with a light joke. They want to understand how you think and if you "get it," meaning you have emotional intelligence. They want to get to the heart of YOU and what's important to you so the recruiter can determine if you will fit the company culture, with the team, and in the role. They also want to know what you

aspire to do. How you answer this question will set the tone for the rest of the conversation.

Substantively, this question is not asking about your equestrian adventures or your last ski trip but at the same time it is asking exactly that. What makes you *you*? What makes you tick? What are your values? What is important to you in the workplace and life? You've already done a values exercise (see chapter 2), so you have a roadmap for what to emphasize. For example, are you a voracious reader? Do you love learning and/or teaching others? Are you the person everyone comes to when they need to solve a problem or someone to talk to who will listen? Do you like to mentor and coach people? Are you good at letting things roll off your back and not get rattled under pressure? Determine the soft skills you have that connect with what is important to you. For example, consider someone who loves to read:

> When I think about my life, the one constant is that I'm a voracious reader. I read pretty much everything I can get my hands on and that has really served me well in learning new areas quickly. I was tapped numerous times in internships to tackle a problem I knew nothing about, but reading, talking to people, asking smart questions, and listening have allowed me to learn anything I don't know but need to know.

In answering this one question, the candidate has already shown an ability to learn, to listen, to take on new challenges, and to adapt. Another example is someone who loves to travel and is applying for a global role that will require travel to a company's offices in Asia:

> I am a lifelong traveler. Learning about new cultures is important to me, and the best way to learn about them is to travel. My last adventure was to Japan, which is an interesting country from a social hierarchy standpoint. It's similar to India in that reputation and manners influence how to work successfully in those countries. That is why I want to work for a global organization because I have the capability to communicate with different cultures in a way that

resonates and I understand how they communicate whether it be high or low context.

By answering the question with a little bit of knowledge about Japan and India, the candidate shows an understanding of cultural differences and how those impact a workplace. For the person who wants to focus on their values and their own fit at a company:

> I have been extremely fortunate to have interned for some amazing managers and incredible companies. That has given me insight into the best work environment for me, which is one that fosters independence, isn't political, and has strong leaders who make decisions quickly after discussion. Through my internships and previous work experience, I have learned that it is hard to find such a great environment. I have heard that your company would match my values and has a culture where I could thrive, and that is why I was so interested in talking with you today about [name of position].

Cultural insight, whether gained in distant lands or in the US, is applicable to every job. That said, you may also have a unique personal history that enhances the conversation.

Alissa from The Winford Group says that some of her most memorable candidates had unusual backgrounds, from running a marathon backward to an obsession with the *New York Times* crossword puzzle. What makes them memorable? "They simply stood out," she said. "I can't tell you anything about people I meet who are serious, bland, and nice because they are forgettable." She advises finding the one thing that makes you interesting and memorable. "We can't all be writers or Olympic athletes, but we can stand out in some unique way, and when there are hundreds of resumes in the pile, that matters."

Don't confuse standing out with getting overly personal. Don't bring up your family, medical illnesses, hardships, or anything negative. Also know that this question is Part 1 of the "story of you." How you answer it, plus the energy and vibe behind it, will either entice the recruiter to want to hear more or end the call early. No pressure!

2. "Can you walk me through your resume?" This sounds like an easy one to answer, but it's not. You should be able to present your resume to a recruiter *in less than two minutes* no matter how many jobs, internships, or volunteer activities you've had. Recruiters aren't asking you to explain everything you did at each company or even talk about each job. They want to hear the highlights of your applicable skills by way of a story, incorporating how you transitioned from job to job or why you chose a specific internship or volunteer opportunity. In talking about each role, they want you to connect the dots about what you've done, what you've learned, and how your experience and knowledge will bring value to the role you are interviewing for. They also want to know the reasons for any gaps on your resume, no matter how small.

Your story should always start with your first job after college or high school if you didn't go to college. The only time you would talk about school is if you were the first in your family to attend one or if there is some other unique fact, such as being the first in five generations to attend a different school than the rest of your family or that your passion for your chosen career began in a specific class (e.g., your passion for marketing began in a subliminal messaging class). Still, any conversation about college should be limited to one or two sentences. For the most part, you will start the conversation with actual work experience.

Work on creating a bold statement for each experience and how that experience connects to the role you are applying for, but don't use obvious phrases such as ". . . and that is similar to the role I'm applying for." When describing positions you've already had, make sure to reference some core concepts from the actual job description. For example (**bold** indicates key words in the job description):

> My first internship was with a small marketing agency where
> I gained understanding and practical experience in **launching
> digital campaigns** and **measuring their outcomes.** From there, I
> knew I wanted to learn more about **product marketing** to round
> out my knowledge of **launching marketing campaigns,** so my
> next internship was with the product marketing team at [name

of company]. There I completed a capstone project where I **conducted market research, met with customers, aligned sales and marketing leadership on product positioning and messaging, created a go-to-market strategy, created marketing collateral, and built out the sales training plan** for what turned out to be a successful launch. When I **measured the adoption rate results and received feedback from the sales team, I analyzed the data** and identified what worked and what didn't, which gave me **insights into providing recommendations** for messaging iterations.

WOW! That one answer incorporates keywords from the job description in a story that tells me this candidate knows the product go-to-market process, participated deeply, understands stakeholder alignment, can accept feedback, and iterate successfully!

If you have had jobs that don't seem to relate to each other—trust me they do. It is your job to connect the dots. Here is an example of how I described my varied experience (**bold** emphasizes key words in the job description and parentheses tell you what I am trying to convey with each statement):

As you can see, I started my career as a TV news reporter. That's where I learned how to **hustle on tight deadlines nightly and hone my written and verbal communication skills,** and where I built my **executive presence** (I can speak to executives). When the internet was taking off, I realized TV news wasn't going to be the only source of news, so I went to night law school while working full-time as a consumer-investigative reporter (hard worker/multitasker). After graduation, I moved to LA to be a screenwriter. We both know how that worked out (humor). That's when I landed a media and legal risk assessment role at NBC, where I vetted reality show participants by reading their background checks and psychological and medical evaluations. You might call me a "psychological profiler" (creating intrigue). That was the beginning of my passion for **understanding people on a deeper level—how they would**

react on set, after the show taped but before it aired, and then after it aired (HR—understanding people).

A former colleague at NBC moved to Viacom and recommended me (I'm good!) for a role there that was broader in scope and responsibility and included **immigration and crew mobility** around the world as well as child labor compliance and managing overall safety on our sets (upgraded role/understanding of HR functions). When my husband took a job in the Bay area, Viacom asked me to stay on (I'm worth it!). I did so for a year and then tried to figure out what I could do with all these skills.

Through the suggestion of a recruiter and a lot of research, I chose HR business partner (new career wasn't a whim but calculated) because I was most successful at NBC and Viacom **strategically helping leaders create successful TV programs by understanding people, which in essence is helping leaders build strong teams of people with the right skills to drive a business and manage people-related issues as they come up on set** (HR skills). I realized I should get certified to prove I understood the nuances of HR, so I took and passed the **SPHR and GPHR** and also spent a full year getting certified in executive **coaching** (HR understanding/ spent time in coaching, not a quick pay for the certificate scam). While I coached a lot in my NBC and Viacom roles, I wanted more tools in my toolkit and I love to learn, so it made sense to complete this certification (capacity to learn).

That is nearly thirty-plus years of work told organically in story form in less than two minutes. Notice that I didn't talk about any one specific accomplishment from my resume. I covered my work history broadly and related it to the role I was applying for (HR business partner) with key words from the job description (in **bold**) in story form. In my last three jobs, I had specific stories or examples of how I brought value to each role in a way that is consistent with the new career. While I had this script in front of me, it was critical that I did not sound like I was reading! After saying it enough, I no longer needed notes. It was my story.

Uncover the parts of *your* story that will add intrigue and personality so the recruiter can get to know you. Your friends know you best; ask them what makes you interesting!

Also notice the transition between jobs. Recruiters want to know the details of what made you leave each role (unless they were just summer internships where it is obvious). If you interned for the same company multiple summers in a row, say that because it indicates they loved your work and wanted you to return. As shown above, my transition statement from NBC to Viacom includes, "A former colleague at NBC moved to Viacom and recommended me for the role . . ." I never worked directly for that colleague, but he was instrumental in me being hired since I didn't initially apply for the role. Giving context for each intentional choice in work experiences builds your credibility.

3. "What interests you about the role at [company name]?" Research. Research. Research. You must do research on a company before taking a recruiter call. You are expected to know enough about the company to sound knowledgeable and to show you put effort into checking it out. I suggest the bare minimum research include the following:

1. Public or private?
2. Who is the CEO? What was their career trajectory? Who is the leader of the department you'd be working in and what was their career trajectory?
3. How many people are in the company?
4. Is the company domestic or worldwide? Where are its offices?
5. What service or product does the company provide?
6. What is the company's Glassdoor rating (be sure to read through the comments)?
7. Read about company culture.
8. Leader or disruptor in its field? Competitive environment?
9. What makes the company unique compared to others in the space?

10. Do you have any relationships with people who work there? If your LinkedIn profile shows such a connection, the recruiter may ask how you know that person.

After doing your research, you should be excited to work at the company for specific reasons. For example:

[company name] is a leader in its industry. It is disrupting the way we do [X]. That type of drive to be number one and stay number one when the competition is fierce describes the company I excel at.

or

I've done some research on the company and talked to a lot of friends who work there [be prepared to name them if asked] and they all say its vision is solid, the culture is fantastic, and the leaders are strong. I'm looking for a company where I believe in the products and the people behind them and I see this role as perfect for my skill set.

or

I am looking for a company that is changing the world. I want to know that the work I do is going to help people in a profound way and [company name] is innovative and doing just that.

The answer to what interests you about a company can be this simple. Don't say, "I have an Amazon Prime membership so it would be fun to work there!" Find a way to show you did your research. At the same time, don't go into detail about the company's products or how it brings in revenue unless the role is related to sales or finance. And while you can usually discover a lot about a company, you won't gain a full understanding of how it does business until you are on the inside.

4. "What is your expectation for compensation?" It may seem odd that a recruiter would ask this so early in the interview process and when you are entering the commercial workforce for the first time, but the last purpose for the recruiter screen is to determine if you and the company are aligned on salary expectations. The most important thing is be ready to answer the question without stumbling.

An important aside: In 2023, the National Partnership for Women and Families found that women made 75 cents for every dollar earned compared to a white, non-Hispanic man for the same job regardless of seniority or job type. Further, people of color continue to experience a gender wage gap. Latinas are paid on average 51 cents and Native American women are paid typically 52 cents for every dollar paid to a white non-Hispanic man. Black women—64 cents.[5] So, if recruiters aren't supposed to ask about compensation, how can they still be asking this question? Because the question is about "expectations" and not actual salary information. As uncomfortable as the question is to so many, it's critical to answer it professionally.

If you provide a salary expectation that's too high, there's a chance a recruiter will decide you have priced yourself out of the role. If you provide one that's too low and you are offered that amount, you will kick yourself later and not feel valued, and it may take years to earn a higher salary or it may require that you move to another company for a new job to catch up. If you decide to ask for more after realizing your mistake, you could come off as untrustworthy or flakey. (See more about negotiating in chapter 15.) Here are some steps to consider when answering this question:

a. Determine the minimum you need to live. Figure out how much money you need to put food on the table, a roof over your head, cover essential needs, with some money for entertainment, etc. Then determine what you think is a fair wage for your experience and the location of the role—a position in San Jose is going to pay more than the same position in Oklahoma City because the cost of labor is much higher in San Jose. Come up with a number without doing any research so you have an idea of what you personally need and want. It doesn't mean you will get this amount but it's important to know if you will need a second job, or whether you are willing to move to a city like New York City if the salary can't meet your needs.

b. Check salary aggregator websites. Research salaries on sites such as Salary.com, Payscale.com, Monster.com, Glassdoor, and Google

Play's salary calculator. Look also at public data through the Bureau of Labor Statistics. Consider reviewing information on the Society for Human Resources Management (SHRM) website or job-specific compensation data from professional and industry associations. And you can always do an online search using the job title and the word "compensation." You'll be surprised at how much public data exists on salaries. Make sure you look at entry-level positions. Cross-referencing is also critical. When I checked some of those sites, the salary differences were surprisingly broad—a lot lower or higher than what I'd been offered in the past. Still, from all this research, you will gain a fairly good idea of what to expect.

c. Talk to people. Talk to friends and colleagues in the same field or reach out to contacts you've made, especially recruiters and those in HR. Any current manager knows the salary ranges of their employees; just don't ask a manager from the same company you are interviewing for as that would be a conflict of interest! Know the level you need to enter—whether that is entry level or one step above if you have a considerable amount of internship or work experience—and make sure you bolster your knowledge and resume to align at that level.

Now that you have all that information and you are fully prepared, do everything you can to not answer the question. You read that right. Do everything you can to answer the question without actually answering it. First, answer the question with a question: "Is there a range for the role?" In California, the company has a legal obligation to provide you the range. The recruiter might say, "I don't have that handy but will get it to you. What range are you hoping for?" You can politely state, "I'd love to hear the range and I'm happy to let you know if we are aligned." Or use one of my favorite lines: "My expectations are negotiable. I want to be fairly compensated for the value I'll bring to the role." If the recruiter provides you a range, you can answer with either "I was thinking the high end of that range is on target" or consider pushing a bit: "That range is slightly lower than what I was expecting but we're close enough that I would love to continue the conversation."

If the range proposed is way too low, try, "Wow, that is a lot lower than I expected." In this instance, either the company doesn't value entry-level employees in your field the way other companies do who pay a higher wage, or a particular industry pays lower than other industries (e.g., entertainment pays less than tech), or the company was simply looking to get a Tesla for the price of a Toyota. If you researched the roles, levels, and salaries and you aren't asking for something far beyond what the market is paying, you need to re-evaluate whether this is the right company, industry, or job level for you.

Although answering a recruiter's questions requires preparation, it is not just about what you say but how you say it. What answers are you most comfortable with and where do you stumble? Confident people don't stammer or over explain. They don't get defensive if the recruiter asks additional questions on a subject you are talking about. They own their decisions and explain how they gained experience, if they took time off, and other choices with confidence. For example, in coaching a student who took off three years before going back to college to care for his ailing father before he passed away knew what he had to say but lacked confidence in saying it because he felt like he should have been able to handle his personal and work life concurrently. Guess what? Life happens. Own it. The best-case scenario is the recruiter realizes your values and priorities are in the right place. Worst-case scenario is they don't get it, but would you want to work for that kind of company anyway? I think not.

Developing a strong sense of presence—knowing who you are and what you are about—will bring the confidence you need to own the decisions you have made in your life. In her book *Presence*, Amy Cuddy writes that presence "is the state of being attuned to and able to comfortably express our true thoughts, feelings, values, and potential."[6] The object is to defeat the thoughts and assumptions that make you feel powerless, thoughts like, "Who will hire me since I have no internship experience in this field because I had to work to support myself in college?" or "I'll never get a job" or "What if I never land that first job?" Cuddy writes about how showing power on the outside can help people overcome how they feel on the inside. She describes "power poses" such as the Wonder Woman pose: hands on hips and your feet slightly apart. She writes, "Let your body tell you that you're powerful and deserving, and you become more present, enthusiastic, and authentically yourself." Stand up and try it. Feel more powerful? More confident? Use that power to answer those four typical interview questions in a way that convinces a recruiter that your career and life choices make you the best candidate for the role.

Be Curious with Questions

Finally, all recruiter screens should end with *you* asking questions. This is your opportunity to learn more about the company but keep your audience in mind. The recruiter has probably set aside 20 to 30 minutes to talk to you. Don't keep them on the phone needlessly even if it's the first recruiter to show interest in you. Ask one or two questions that a recruiter can answer. Don't ask detailed questions about the day-to-day responsibilities of the job itself because the recruiter likely doesn't know. Save those questions for the hiring manager. During a recruiter screen, consider simple closing questions such as:

→ "What makes people successful at [company name]?"

→ "I did some research on the culture, but can you give me an example of the way culture is embodied at the company?"

→ "What has the hiring manager said is the most important skill for this role?"

→ "What intangible skills are you looking for in this role?"

→ "Is this role new or a backfill?" If backfill, "How has the role evolved since the last person held the position?"

→ "Are there any other questions I can answer that will help you believe I am the perfect fit for this role?"

→ "What is the interview process like from here at [company name]?"

→ "I'm very interested in the role you described. If I'm fortunate enough to move to the next round, what is the process?"

By asking that last question, you will know where you are in the process if you receive a transparent answer. If you don't get past a recruiter screen, chalk it up to not being the right fit in hard or soft skills or in culture. Or the recruiter may sense you aren't being authentic. Recruiters don't want some mythical version of you—they want *you*. If you are selling yourself the entire time and not paying attention to where the conversation is heading or you can't turn off the "interview version" of you, the recruiter may pass before you get a chance to talk to the hiring manager. Therefore, answer each question with authenticity and showing some personality that will allow a recruiter to determine if you are truly a viable candidate for the role and the company.

Chapter 13 Summary

1. **Take every recruiter call:** Build a relationship with every recruiter because you never know if a recruiter will present you with an incredible opportunity now or in the future.

2. **Research the recruiter:** Know if you are you talking to an internal or external recruiter and the kind of company that is interested in you.

3. **Know the purpose of the recruiter screen:** A recruiter's screen is meant to explain the role, describe the company, make sure you have the foundational hard/soft skills for the role, determine whether you are a culture fit for the company, and understand your overall interest in the role by the end of the conversation.

4. **Prepare answers to the typical four questions:** Write down two-minute answers to the four questions recruiters usually

ask using key words from the job description that directly connect your experience to the career you want to enter.

5. **Exude confidence:** Be confident in your answers; practice before every call.

14

Beyond the Recruiter Screen

"Before anything else, preparation is the key to success."
—Alexander Graham Bell, inventor, scientist

If you didn't make it through the recruiter screen, try to get feedback from the recruiter as to why. Most of the time you will receive the proverbial, "We had candidates who better matched what we were looking for." But if you've built a relationship with the recruiter and you take the rejection well, sometimes you'll get some useful feedback. Simply ask, "I understand there are a lot of great candidates out there. I am going to interview with other companies, so any feedback you can give on my interview with you would be most helpful." While many companies and recruiters are scared in this litigious society of being sued for discrimination for their feedback, they may still provide some insight that will explain their decision and help you in the future.

If you made it through the recruiter screen, celebrate! That is a huge accomplishment. But as they say, now the real work begins. You will win or lose the job in the next round of interviews.

No matter how much I tried to make candidates feel comfortable while interviewing them in my role as a hiring manager, I know they weren't. There you are, sitting either in person or via video, in front of the person who is deciding during a 30- to 45-minute interview whether you have a future at their company. The more a

Tip #14: Prepare, prepare, and prepare some more.

candidate wants the job, the more uncomfortable some become. I have seen extroverts turn into introverts. I have seen people sweat, shake, and clasp their hands so tight their fingers turn red. Even I get nervous. I am pretty loud in general, which could be off-putting to some, but I've also been so nervous when interviewing for a new job that my bubbly personality almost becomes too stiff.

Fortunately, interviewing doesn't have to be horrible! In fact, most companies are fighting for the right candidates (especially during times of low unemployment), so if they are working hard to recruit you, you should work just as hard to gain their faith and show why you are the best candidate. And it doesn't matter if you are interviewing in person or via video. Via video, only two things change: the location and whether you can have notes in front of you.

If you are interviewing via video, make sure you have a well-lit location. Consider what is in your background. Is it warm and inviting? Will it make people feel uncomfortable? I suggest not having a bed or toilet in your background if at all possible. You can always add a virtual background. Also, a wall right behind you may cause you to cast a shadow. Adhere to the rule of thirds by positioning your head in the upper third and fill most of the screen with your shoulders, not background. Don't show lower than your torso. When interviewing, if you are interrupted by a siren, a roommate, or a gardener, simply apologize once and let it go.

While interviewing via video may seem less personal, an advantage to interviewing from home is you can have notes. I would never recommend bringing notes to an in-person interview, but at home, no one can see if you have notes, as long as you don't sound like you are reading and you don't shift your eyes continuously toward your notes, which can make you look untrustworthy. If you get nervous and forget what you want to cover during interviews, consider taping a sheet of paper with a few short bullet points to the wall just past the camera lens. No matter where you are interviewing, the key is to listen carefully and answer the exact question being asked succinctly and thoroughly while showing some personality to help the interviewer understand if they would enjoy working with you every day.

Positioning Your Work

Resumes open doors; interviewing closes them. The question is, which side will you be on when they close? Thus, how you position your experience and skills is critical. But how can you do that if you don't know what they will ask? The good news is that you don't need to know the questions. You do need to prepare answers that will fit any and all questions asked. For example, here are five common interview questions from hiring managers:

→ "What accomplishment are you most proud of?"

→ "Tell me about a time when you had to prioritize multiple projects?"

→ "Tell me about a time when you had to influence the direction of a project?

→ Tell me about a time you failed and how did you recover?

→ "What are your strengths and what areas do you need to develop (aka weaknesses)?

These seem like totally different questions, but you could handle them all with one answer if your greatest accomplishment was influencing a leader on how to solve a business problem after a few attempts that failed and getting buy-in from stakeholders before rolling it out. But you will need at least one unique story for each of these questions. Here is how to draft a relevant story that aligns with the job description.

Step 1: Review the job description and think about all the big career accomplishments that stand out in your mind that **relate to the job description and the new job.** What makes your examples accomplishments? Did you complete a big project? Did you have to get stakeholder buy-in? Now, take five big accomplishments that are directly applicable to the job description and prepare five different examples of your work using the STAR method.

Reminder: The STAR method is Situation, Task, Action, Result. **Situation** is the "what"—the challenge or business problem that needed to be solved. It is best to present a challenge you identified, or found yourself in, and you were charged with coming up with the solution. Don't describe a situation that someone else was in and you came in and "saved the day." Those examples may be viable but describing them may come off as arrogant if not positioned well. **Task** describes the goal or what you needed to achieve. When will you know a solution is in place and working? **Action** is the "how" you did the work to bring about the solution and reach the goal. This is the perfect spot to describe soft skills. **Results** are the outcomes and measurement of those outcomes. When interviewing, add a T for **Takeaways** as well—STAR(T). Takeaways are short statements about what you learned from the experience and how you incorporated that learning into future work. By concluding with a takeaway, it shows growth and learning from the experience.

When discussing issues in the STAR method, it is important to use the word "I" even if you are describing a team project. It is fine to use "we" at times, but make sure the interviewer knows what you did specifically to solve the issue. Otherwise, the interviewer won't know if you personally know how to do the work or if you were just an observer. Own what you did! Here is an example of a college graduate's answer to "Tell me about your greatest accomplishment." She had numerous internships in business operations:

SITUATION: What business problem needed to be solved?

Problem: When I was interning at [company name], the company was struggling to efficiently allocate resources across its various departments, leading to bottlenecks in workflow and decreased productivity. I was tasked with finding a solution to optimize resource allocation and streamline operations.

TASK: What would help that **Situation** change and how did you come up with a solution?

Goal: In talking to stakeholders and diving deep into the issue, it was clear early in my research that we needed a new resource allocation strategy that would effectively distribute resources across departments, prioritize projects based on their importance and urgency in alignment with company goals, and ensure optimal utilization of valuable resources which are critical to the company's continued success and growth.

ACTION: What actions did you take to change the Situation and in what order? Hold brainstorming meetings? Influence stakeholder buy-in? Collaborate closely with cross-functional co-workers? Did you motivate your team? (Don't forget to include your soft skills here!)

Actions taken: I began by conducting thorough research into best practices for resource allocation and operational efficiency within similar tech startups. I analyzed the company's current workflow, identified pain points, and interviewed key stakeholders to better understand their needs and challenges. Drawing on my coursework and previous internship experiences, I devised a comprehensive resource allocation model that leveraged data analytics and automation to allocate resources dynamically.

To implement this solution, I had to first align and influence stakeholders that this was the best option. Then I collaborated closely with the company's IT and finance teams to identify a new resource allocation system, and worked with a project manager on the integration of the new system with existing software platforms and financial systems. I also drafted and implemented a change management plan and organized training sessions to ensure a smooth transition and foster buy-in for the new process.

RESULTS: What were the results of your efforts?

Measurable outcomes: The new model, including the workflow and system, significantly improved the company's operational efficiency and productivity. By prioritizing projects based on strategic objectives and resource availability, the new system reduced bottlenecks by 50%, eliminated unnecessary delays, and enhanced cross-departmental collaboration. As a result, the company was better positioned to capitalize on growth opportunities and maintain its competitive edge in the market.

TAKEAWAYS: What did you learn and how did you grow from this experience?

Learnings/Change: Through this experience, I honed my problem-solving capabilities through each phase of the project. I also researched and implemented change management strategies for the first time and saw first-hand the value of effective change management in driving organizational change and fostering alignment across different functional areas.

With at least five examples crystalized in this format, nearly any question can be answered about your work experience. Try to incorporate both hard and soft skills in each example and use at least one example to focus on soft skills, specifically communication, time management, flexibility, or trust. This will reveal your ability to juggle multiple projects (time management), switch gears on the fly (flexibility), and/or build relationships (trust).

Step 2: Now take these examples and create stories with a beginning, middle, and end using the STAR(T) method. Add some personality and take out information that dives too deeply into the details. Each story should be no longer than two minutes. That's why it's important to write them down and practice so you can prevent sidebars or unimportant details from slowing things down. Once you feel comfortable, you'll have five key stories to choose from for any of the obvious questions and the confidence to deliver them.

Strengths and Weaknesses

Questions regarding your strengths and weaknesses may seem antiquated, but some interviewers will still ask about these "areas for development." They may also ask what you are doing to improve them. The goal of this question is to determine if you are self-aware enough to know where you are strong and what you need to work on. But this question can also be a "trap" and be used against you if you answer it the wrong way. Claiming you are a perfectionist and never make mistakes is hubris. The weakness should be something you have already overcome or are actively working on. By owning your weakness, you are showing self-awareness and the ability to adapt and change. And everyone has a weakness. The goal is to answer the question directly and with confidence—itself a soft skill.

Most people find it easier to come up with strengths than a "positive sounding" weakness. Some strengths examples include team player, flexible or adaptable to new areas or change, remaining calm in the face of pressure, critical/creative thinker, superior communicator, effective manager or leader who can motivate and empower, problem solver, resourceful, influencer (not the online kind), public speaker, ability to learn quickly. Pick a strength that aligns with the job description requirements and qualifications. Make sure you have a story in case they ask how you use your strengths at work.

Weaknesses or "areas for development" that don't make you sound like a bad employee are harder to come up with. It can also be challenging to explain a weakness without stumbling. Practicing this answer is just as important as practicing all the others. The key is making sure you explain how you've improved and/or are turning those weaknesses into strengths. Here are some examples of "positive" weaknesses:

→ I tend to raise my hand for exciting new projects even if I don't have the bandwidth, but I've gotten better at letting others have some of those opportunities because I can learn from supporting other's successes as much as doing it myself. For example, . . . (Add two sentences on a project you gave up and what you learned from the other person's accomplishment.)

→ In my first two internships, I wasn't exposed to all the ways that data can be used, and it's been a learning curve. Now I think about data at the start of every project while learning new ways to track results. I'd say I'm proficient but there is still more to learn. (Add two sentences about your success using data but also how you now lean on others with specific expertise before starting a new project to make sure you are not missing something.)

→ I'm a critical observer, so when I'm in a large meeting, I tend to listen to everyone else before speaking because I like to hear all the sides and analyze the points being made. Sometimes I don't speak at all if my opinion has been voiced by someone else. I still listen, but now I'm more apt to speak up to make sure my voice is heard when I have an important point to make or information to add to the conversation. (Add two sentences about a recent meeting where when you spoke up and your point was used to catapult a decision or a new way of doing something.)

Notice how the weaknesses really aren't weaknesses, but great qualities to have in an employee. The goal is to add two sentences after each weakness showing your improvement or your own self-awareness of the weakness and steps you are taking to make sure your weakness is not prohibiting your success.

Connecting the Dots

If you make that second interview, the recruiter believes you have some skills and the hiring manager is interested in talking with you based on the recruiter's feedback. Your mission is to keep connecting all the dots. Because this is your first job, some hard skills may be missing, such as specific software experience. If you are short on hard skills based on the job description, focus on your soft skills; they are applicable to any job you apply for. Nearly every job requires effective communication skills, strong presentation skills, accountability, time-management skills, and an ability to work in fast-paced or slower-paced environments. The examples you give in the STAR(T) method should highlight those skills that are directly applicable to the job you want.

One of my favorite soft-skill stories I told during interviews was about an A-list singer who wouldn't perform at a major event if she couldn't fly her unmanned drone over the audience and on to the stage to open the show. This represented a huge potential liability, but she was the opening act. The goal was to tell her she couldn't do it but in a way that would still ensure she would show up and perform on opening night. I came up with a solution using FAA **research** and by **leveraging relationships** at the studio. Then I **coached** senior leaders, including the **president** of the cable channel, on what to say to her. We worked it out; she did perform, and it was a win all around. While this was not a situation I would ever have to deal with in HR, it showed I was solution-oriented and could influence leaders with sound advice on how to deal with difficult people in a tense situation. And it was an intriguing story that stands out! You want to be interesting and remembered.

What Questions to Ask

Nearly every interviewer will ask, "Do you have any questions?" And you better have some or you will look like you haven't thought about the job or the company, which will suggest you aren't that interested. Bob Hancock has recruited thousands of people in his career and the one negative he hears over and over from hiring managers is that a candidate had no questions. "It does play in the hiring decision," he said. "Having questions shows you did some research and are curious about the company or the team you would join. Not having any questions gives all hiring managers pause and may lose you the job."

Examples of questions to ask:

→ **To the hiring manager:** What is your management style? How do you keep up on what your team members are doing? What is the one thing the last person in this job could have done better? What happened to the last person in this role? How do you provide feedback to your team members? How would you set expectations for the role if I'm fortunate enough to be chosen for this job? What defines success in this role? What one area of the company or within the group do you think could be improved? Why do you like working for [company name]?

→ **To additional interviewers:** Tell me how the company or group has changed during your time here? What one thing would make someone successful in this role? How do you see the person in this role interacting with your function/role? Can you give me a better understanding of the culture here? Would you consider this a fast- or slow-paced decision-making environment and can you give me an example? Why do you like working for [company name]? If there is one unwritten rule at this company that everyone eventually figures out, what would that be? What is your best piece of advice for someone onboarding here?

If those don't work for you or you are having trouble coming up with interview questions, check out John Kador's *301 Best Questions to Ask on Your Interview*. Reminder: You are allotted a certain amount of time to meet with each interviewer. They likely have another meeting right after yours or another interviewer is waiting at the door. Most interviewers don't want to stay one minute over no matter how much they like you. Therefore, if you are going to ask questions, don't wait until your time is up.

Be careful about asking questions that could be misinterpreted. For example, "How late do people work?" or "Do people work remotely?" or "How much vacation time do people get?" may suggest to them that you are lazy, won't put in the time needed, or are expecting to work from home before proving yourself in the role. Even if having such flexibility or a certain amount of vacation time is part of your values, ask the question in a way that doesn't leave a negative impression. "Tell me about the overall benefits and the company's position on work schedules" is a much more diplomatic approach. Further, hold such questions until later in the recruiting process—don't ask the hiring manager. The recruiter will know the company's culture and have those answers, and since you have already built a relationship with them, they will be less likely to misinterpret the questions.

Prepare Your Psyche

Now that you've established your stories and skills and your thoughts are clear, it's time to prepare your psyche. Walking into an interview should be akin to a football player running on the field to play in a big game: You need the energy and excitement that tells you, "I've got this!" To that end, I recommend the following:

1. **Quiet time before the interviews.** Arrive at the interview site at least 30 minutes prior, park down the block for 15 minutes, and clear your head of the day's craziness. If it is a video call, take the 30 minutes prior to focus. Meditation is great, but if you aren't into that or fear it will mellow you out too much, simply bring your notes and focus on your stories.

2. **Music to pump you up.** I'm a big believer of playing a song that energizes you—not the one that gets stuck in your head but the song that makes you want to tap your feet or get your dance on. For me it's "Don't Stop Me Now" (Queen), "Confident" (Demi Lovato), "Just Like Fire" (Pink), "Fighter" (Christina Aguilera), or anything Lizzo like "Good as Hell." Get your energy up and your groove on.

3. **Power pose.** If you're at home prior to the interview or you find a bathroom in the building where the interview will be, bring on that Amy Cuddy "Wonder Woman" stance. That's right: Hands on hips. Legs strong. Head held high. The stance that once again says, "I've got this!"

Chapter 14 Summary

1. **Pick five great accomplishments:** Review the job description and list five career accomplishments where you used both hard and soft skills that relate to the job description and the new job.

2. **STAR(T) Method:** Using the STAR(T)—Situation, Task, Action, Result, (Takeaway)—method, create stories around those five accomplishments that incorporate the hard and soft skills needed for the job.

3. **Strengths and Weaknesses:** Identify your strengths and how you've leveraged them and how you have improved upon or overcome your weaknesses.

4. **Ask questions:** Ask the hiring manager smart questions to show interest in the role.

5. **Psych yourself up:** Get yourself in the right headspace for the interview. Meditate, say affirmations, play music, do a power pose—whatever works before you start the interview.

The Hiring Process

"Patience and fortitude conquer all things."

—Ralph Waldo Emerson, American essayist

You may have finished your in-person interviews, but the process isn't over until you start the job. When you are looking for a new job, it is all consuming and top-of-mind *for you*. But the hiring manager is still doing his day job while trying to make the right hire. You are not the hiring manager's sole focus of the day, week, or even month. And a lot happens behind the scenes.

Summary of the Hiring Process

1. A job is posted.

2. The recruiter or hiring manger will search for potential candidates on LinkedIn to "calibrate" the type of experience and profile the hiring manager expects.

3. The recruiter looks through the first fifty resumes of those who applied to see if anyone has the right experience for the position.

4. The recruiter either screens a few candidates or presents first-glance candidates to the hiring manager to determine who to pursue.

5. The recruiter completes screening interviews.

6. The recruiter and hiring manager meet or exchange emails to discuss what was learned from the screening interviews.

7. The hiring manager decides if any of the candidates should move to the next round.

8. The recruiter schedules the hiring manager to meet with one or several candidates over the next few days or weeks.

9. The hiring manager does a phone screen with the candidate or, if possible, the candidate is brought on site.

10. The hiring manager and recruiter debrief over which, if any, candidate should move forward in the process.

11. The recruiter schedules the next round of interviews.

12. The hiring manager interviews top candidates on site (if possible) for a second time. Additional interviewers are brought in and/or the candidate is asked to give a presentation.

13. The recruiter, hiring manager, and anyone else who interviewed the candidate debrief on what they learned and whether the candidate has the right skills for the role and will fit within the culture of the company and the team.

14. The hiring manager decides who will move to the next round or if the recruiter should search for new candidates, in which case the process starts over.

15. Candidates who move forward likely come back for a final round of interviews.

16. The hiring manager and interviewers debrief.

17. If a candidate moves toward offer, the hiring manager or recruiter checks references.

18. The recruiter works with the hiring manager and compensation leaders to determine an appropriate offer and they decide who will present it.

19. The offer is presented verbally to the candidate followed by an offer letter.

20. Negotiation may ensue, but note, if this is truly your first job, you don't have a lot of negotiating power.

21. Anything outside the standard compensation package for the level and title will need approval from senior leaders including the hiring manager's boss, finance, and HR.

22. Once there's agreement on the compensation package, the candidate is given a small window of time to sign the offer letter.

23. The candidate signs and a hire is made.

Tip #15: Be patient with the hiring process, which may not fit into your timeline.

The process for each hiring manager is just that—a process—and no two job interview processes will be the same. The goal is to stay in the process without missteps. And an offer is almost always contingent on a background check; that additional paperwork will be sent to the candidate upon acceptance. The entire process can take from two to four months or even longer, so if you made it to the end, congratulate yourself!

Scams

Understanding the hiring process will help you avoid becoming a victim of employment scams. Unfortunately, hiring scams have become increasingly prevalent in the job market, posing significant risks to newly graduated job seekers. These scams often involve fraudulent job postings, promising lucrative opportunities or work-from-home positions with minimal effort. Scammers may impersonate legitimate companies, using similar websites and email addresses to deceive applicants.

Common red flags include requests for personal financial information such as bank account or social security numbers, upfront payments for training or equipment, and vague job descriptions with promises of high earnings. You will never be asked for your social security number or personal financial information as you move through the interview process with any legitimate employer. When you fill out your background check, the background check company will send you an online application where you will be asked for your social security number, date of birth, previous addresses over the past seven-to-ten years, and previous names, if you have used aliases. It is crucial for job seekers to remain vigilant and conduct thorough research on prospective employers, verifying their legitimacy through colleagues, mentors, or friends.

Another red flag I hear is how some companies will tell candidates they are finalists and then ask them to execute a project. Some companies provide a specific situation or analysis to assess a candidate's thought process or work product. Too often, however, candidates provide the work thinking they are shoe-ins for the job only to never hear from the company again. You just got swindled for free work! And yet how could you say no? In such an instance, I suggest asking instead if you can present a project you completed in the past. If the answer is no, ask if you can present some ideas in verbal form only (without any leave-behind documentation). If you've done such projects in the past and that work was never acknowledged but you saw some of the results executed on the open market, let them know. It justifies your hesitation.

Thank-you Notes

Once you are in the process, you want to stay in the process! Therefore, after you finish the in-person interviews, write thank-you notes. Use the opportunity to provide more context about your skills and keep your name top of mind. Back in the '90s and early 2000s, candidates wrote handwritten thank-you notes and sent them via US postal service (aka "snail mail"). Some people still rely on handwritten thank-you notes, and while noble, the hiring process moves quickly and it may take days for that note to arrive. Further, with more people working from home, interviewers may never receive a thank-you note that is sent to the office. The hiring manager may assume you didn't write one and lean toward another more etiquette savvy candidate. Bob says he's floored at how many candidates don't write thank-you notes: "By not writing a thank-you note, you are sending a message to me and the hiring manager that you are not proactive or not interested in the role."

While that narrative may not be true for everyone, forgetting this step could torpedo your candidacy. I once heard a recruiter comment that if a candidate couldn't write a simple note, they couldn't be trusted with company business. Fortunately, email is fine. Make sure you at least get one business card if you interviewed in person or you ask the recruiter for the company email address format (e.g., first name.last name @company.com). As a last resort, ask the recruiter to forward your thank-you notes to the respective interviewers for you. Thank-you notes can be simple, but they should also connect the dots between you and the job and/or cover something that you discussed. Some examples:

> Thank you so much for taking the time to meet with me today. I left even more excited about the role, thinking about how I can add value to the team overall and be a successful collaborator in your complex organization. My experience in [X] and [Y], combined with my insatiable curiosity to learn, will help me be successful as a [job title] on your dynamic team.
>
> Thank you again and I look forward to hearing from you soon.

or

> Thank you for taking the time to interview me today. I really enjoyed our conversation. It was great to hear your perspective on company culture, expectations on accountability, and the incredibly talented people I would be collaborating with should I be fortunate to secure this role. My experience and ability to learn quickly would allow me to bring a diverse perspective to the role of [title] on your culturally diverse team.
>
> I hope we'll be working together in the near future.

or

> Thank you for taking the time to interview me today. I am
> excited about the possibility of working with your senior leaders
> on [A, B, and C]. My experience, combined with my ability to learn
> quickly, will allow me to hit the ground running.
>
> If you have any further questions about my background, please
> don't hesitate to ask. I look forward to hearing from you soon.

What if you bombed one of the interviews? You were asked questions about process and you answered with personal stories. Or you stammered through answers. Put a positive spin on them in the thank-you note:

> Thank you for taking the time to interview me today. While
> I didn't feel I expressed myself as clearly as I could have on some
> of your questions, I know I'll be able to bring value to the areas we
> discussed including [A, B, and/or C] if given the opportunity. My
> excitement for working at [company name] is even stronger after
> meeting with your stellar team today.

or

> Thank you for taking the time to interview me today. I am
> excited about the possibility of working with your senior leaders
> on [A, B, and C]. My experience, combined with my ability to learn
> quickly, will allow me to hit the ground running.
>
> I thought more about the question you asked me about
> providing an example of a growth mindset. I stumbled in the room
> but thought of dozens of examples on the way home including [A
> and B]. As a naturally analytical person, I like to think deeply about
> questions and provide thorough and thoughtful answers. I hope
> that helps explain my thought process more clearly.
>
> If you have any further questions about my background, please
> don't hesitate to ask. I look forward to hearing from you soon.

These notes address the issue you had but also reinforce the value you would bring to the company. Thank-you notes, like references, may seem like a "formality" but they are part of the hiring process. Leverage your thank-you notes to reiterate the connection between your current skills and those required in the job description while emphasizing your ability to learn quickly.

References

If you haven't received an offer yet but you've been asked for references, there's a good chance you are one of two finalists. Your references may then determine whether you get the job. If you have already received an offer, it could be contingent on your references and a background check.

Every job, whether you love it or hate it, is a place to build relationships with people who could one day sing your praises. A reference will tell a prospective manager at a new company or even the one you work for about your strengths and development areas, your work style, and whether you'd fit in with the culture of the company or team you are trying to join. The best way to ensure your references say something nice about you is to be a top performer with exceptional hard and soft skills. Simple! The more enthusiastic the reference, the better chance you have at securing a job.

Step 1: Choosing the Right References

The first step is to find at least three people who are willing to give you a positive reference. Then ask them on the phone or in person if they are comfortable being an enthusiastic reference. Any hesitation means the person is not comfortable even if they don't say so out loud. Never provide a hesitant reference to a prospective employer. Why? Only part of the equation is saying great things about you; the other part is the enthusiasm behind the great things. Enthusiasm is especially important because recruiters and hiring managers will pick up on a tentative or hesitant reference.

I once had a former employee reach out and ask me for a reference. This employee was not a high performer and left my team shortly before being fired. I knew this employee had worked in a few other roles since working for me and there was no way I could give a positive and enthusiastic reference. So, I simply said, "I don't think I can give you the enthusiastic reference you need since you haven't worked for me in a few years." Unfortunately, some people think it is easier to just say "Sure" even if they have misgivings, and those references may come back to haunt you.

If everyone you contact is enthusiastic, who do you choose to be a reference? Most recruiters will ask the reference how they know you, so choose managers or colleagues with whom you have worked closely.

Former/current manager. This person is the ideal reference because former or current managers can tell a prospective employer how you brought value to the team, what projects you worked on, how you built relationships, how you worked cross-functionally, and how you succeeded in the role. However, most job seekers don't want to use a current manager in case the new role at the new company doesn't work out, and that makes sense. Also, if a current manager does give you a reference, some potential employers may wonder if that manager is trying to unload you due to poor performance unless there are special circumstances such as a merger/acquisition, reduction in force, or other issues. But do ask a former manager or supervisor to be an enthusiastic reference if you left on good terms. If you happen to be working, always alert your current manager before applying for a new internal position. You will not want your current manager to hear about your application from a colleague before you explained why you applied for the other role.

Colleagues/co-workers/fellow interns. Former or current colleagues can be exceptional references, especially if they worked directly with you on a complex, cross-functional project. Seek out the highest-titled colleague who is willing to provide you that enthusiastic reference because title means credibility. A co-worker or fellow intern can also lend their support if you worked with them closely on a project.

Customers/clients. If you work in a customer service–type role and you have a recurring customer, or you work in sales and have clients, consider them as references, especially if they can speak to your ability to solve problems, influence, persuade, and build relationships.

Networking colleagues/college professors. References who haven't actually worked with you are considered character references. They can talk about who you are as a person, such as "Everyone loves [your name]" or "[your name] is a hard worker." Try to find someone you worked with in a school activity or committee who can speak to your win-win skills. College students sometimes use professors as references. They can acknowledge that you are a top performer or class leader but can't usually provide insights on real-world experience unless you were a research assistant or worked for them. These references are not as effective as former managers or colleagues who connect the dots from your work to the job you are applying for. Networking colleagues and college professors should be the last option if you can't find more relevant references.

Family and friends. No! Don't use them as a reference even if you worked for a family business. Find someone else in that business or provide a reference from another job. For example, if you work for your dad's business and he is the CEO, ask the next highest person for a reference. The last thing you want is a recruiter asking, "How do you know the candidate?" and your reference answers, "Oh, he's my son!"

Step 2: Preparing References

When I was a manager, I was always shocked when candidates didn't alert their references they were applying for a new role. I would call references and they would ask how the candidate was doing because they hadn't heard from them in a while, or the reference would ask what job the candidate was applying for at what company. It is a lost opportunity if you don't prepare your references to say the right things to help you secure the role. At a minimum, you should make sure they know the following:

a. The job you are interviewing for (provide the job description).

b. Information you were unable or forgot to explain in the interview process that would be helpful to the hiring manager. For example, that you are comfortable working in an ambiguous environment (with an example). Or you are a quick learner (provide an example). Or you are good at digging deep to understand a problem before offering solutions (again, with an example). You may need to remind your reference of your accomplishments and value so they have examples to provide to the recruiter.

c. What skill set is critical for the role and how specific skills you either have or learned in your current career or position transfer directly to the role you are applying to. Provide examples.

d. Qualities that make you a great candidate for the role.

e. Qualities that make you unique out of all the other possible candidates out there. This is where your "unique perspective" on the role comes in and how you have been successful jumping into projects or roles where you knew nothing when you started.

f. Weaknesses or areas for development that you have worked hard to overcome (e.g., you had trouble pivoting on a project after receiving feedback but you no longer hold onto previous direction and are able to pivot much easier).

g. The importance that their enthusiasm will play in influencing the hiring team.

Discuss the above with all references and/or send bullet points for them to review prior to giving their contact information to a prospective employer.

Step 3: Handling Backdoor References

Some employers no longer ask for references because they know candidates will provide only those who say positive things about them, often with scripted answers. Instead, some employers seek "backdoor" references, meaning someone who has worked with the candidate but isn't on a candidate's reference list. Those types of references can be more genuine in their characterization of a candidate or less genuine if they had a direct conflict with the candidate.

When backdoor references are negative, I tend to dig deeper as a hiring manager and ask, "How long ago did you two work together?" Then I will follow up with, "Do you know anyone else who feels the same way?" I'll ask for specific names and contact information for anyone mentioned. If the reference worked with the candidate more than five years ago and can't provide other people who feel the same way to corroborate their opinion or I'm told the candidate "managed up" well so no one else had a conflict, I am much less willing to rely heavily on their information. Why? People can grow and change from previous experiences. Unfortunately, not everyone is so forgiving.

More than twenty years ago, when I was a TV news reporter, I lost two potential jobs because a former boss gave a negative backdoor reference. How did I know? One recruiter disappeared—commonly known as "ghosting" (more about ghosting on page 191)—the day after I was told an offer would be coming. None of my references told me the recruiter called them, but the recruiter apparently had called other people I had worked with, including, I presume, my former boss. The other recruiter slipped and admitted, "We got some information and realized you wouldn't be a good fit here." That was my first lesson about relationships and that it doesn't matter if you have great accomplishments—negative behavior will linger in the minds of others. It also taught me that my behavior in my twenties was going to haunt me if I didn't do something about it.

I was immature back then but becoming more self-aware and working on myself and my behavior. The bad news was that no one knew I had grown and changed since my first few jobs. I decided to write a letter (no email back then) to that former news director explaining how I had matured, how I would have handled events differently, and how I would hate to be judged in the future for actions in my early twenties. I never heard back, but I also never had a problem securing a job again.

The best way to ensure that everyone you work with has something positive to say about you is to build relationships. Find your champions in every job who know your value. If you notice relationships suffering because you may have offended someone or didn't show your best side, consider a mea culpa even if you believe the other person is wrong. Would you rather be content or contentious? Would you rather be right or employed in your dream job? You can't stop someone from saying something bad about you, but you can grow from every experience and show your growth in the next opportunity.

Silence

If you were asked for references, that is usually the last step before potentially getting an offer. But many companies ask more than one candidate for references. It can take weeks to do reference checks and decide if you are the person the company wants to hire. All that waiting may create a dialogue in your head about what your references are saying or wishing you said something different in the interview stage. I remember saying to my husband days before I received an offer from Roku that I was sad I hadn't heard from the recruiter and I guess I didn't get the job. You may start to question your ability to do the job or convince yourself the company chose someone else. It is amazing what those six inches between your ears can do to your confidence! If you are waiting in silence, it usually means one of two things:

1. You're #2. The company made an offer to the top-choice candidate first. That may feel like failure but it's not. You made it to #2! That's actually amazing! That means it's just a matter of time before you become a hiring manager's top candidate. You have no idea if someone was referred to the company, whether an internal person is a candidate looking to transition to the role, or the top candidate's skills are no different from yours, but they had internships in the same industry and you don't.

When I interviewed for an HR business partner role to support the chief medical officer, the recruiter told me I was a finalist for the role with two other people. Then it was down to me and one other person.

The person hired had supported a chief medical officer in a previous role in a med-tech company. I could boast neither of those. Not only that, the hiring manager was also moving into a new role supporting the chief medical officer and other senior leaders. While strategic HR business partnering is similar in most tech companies, I understood why the other candidate was hired; his experience would allow him to ramp up the hiring manager quicker on how that side of the business works.

I expressed my disappointment and asked to be considered for future opportunities. That was my way of asking for feedback or determining if my candidacy was over at that company for good. I had made it to the end and wanted to hear what I could have done better or what I could learn from the experience. "You belong here," the executive recruiter said. "We just had someone who had experience supporting a chief medical officer. But one of the people you interviewed with is about to have an opening and she'd like to continue the conversation with you." That may sound like a "line," but a few weeks later, the new hiring manager called me, we grabbed coffee, and she hired me a few months later. And the person they hired for the first role? I met him my first day of work in the cafeteria and immediately realized why he was hired for the previous role. It wasn't just his experience, but his calm demeanor. My bubbly personality worked better with a sales organization. That's why you need to stay positive and use every interview experience to hone your message so when a hiring manager is ready to take a risk, you are ready.

2. Ghosting. Unfortunately, the other reason why you may not have heard back from a company is called "ghosting." I don't condone this rude behavior, but it can happen at any point in the process once the recruiting process has started. While it would be nice to have closure, if a company loses interest at any point in the process, you may never hear another word. What did you do wrong? Maybe your initial screen or the panel interviews didn't go as well as you thought, your references weren't as enthusiastic as the other finalists, or the company got an unflattering backdoor reference. Sometimes headcount gets reallocated to another role, the job description changed based on business needs, or the company decided to hire internally. Sometimes two external recruiters are working to fill the same position and the one you're not talking to found the perfect candidate. There are lots of reasons that could have nothing to do with you—and you may never know why.

How do you find out if you've been ghosted and the process didn't stall due to the hiring manager's unexpected illness? Check in via email or phone call. It's painless. Just don't have expectations. If a company is really interested in a candidate, it will normally keep the candidate "warm," meaning the recruiter or hiring manager will stay in contact with updates. After two emails or voicemail follow-ups, it is time to let go. A company that doesn't even give you a courtesy call or email to let you know you are no longer being considered isn't a company you will want to work for anyway. Time to play Taylor Swift's "Shake It Off" and move on.

On the flip side, the ancient proverb "Two wrongs don't make a right" comes to mind. If you've been ghosted in the past, that's no reason to ghost a potential employer during the interview process or after you have an offer! Once you have engaged in the interview process and taken the recruiter screen, you have an obligation to let the recruiter know if you want to be removed from the process. Disappearing leaves a bad impression and can make the recruiter look bad, especially if you have already been pitched as a candidate to the hiring manager.

I remember a candidate who filled out all their pre-employment paperwork and was scheduled to arrive at headquarters his first day but never showed up. No call. No email. I watched the recruiter try in vain to reach the candidate via phone and email with no response. After a day of attempts, the recruiter asked the local police to do a welfare check. One knock on their door confirmed the candidate was fine. He then wrote a nasty email to the recruiter saying he had simply changed his mind about the role, that the recruiter went too far sending the police to his house, and to "chill out." WHAT?! Yes, that recruiter's caring about someone's well-being apparently went "too far." It takes a simple phone call to say you are no longer interested, changed your mind, have another offer, or that something else came up. Much better than the police showing up at your house!

And remember: Recruiters move! Hiring managers move! And they both have long memories.

You Get an Offer

Not all hiring processes end in rejection. Sometimes you get an offer! You have three ways to respond:

1. Accept immediately.

2. Say you are incredibly excited about the opportunity and would love to review the paperwork and will respond on a specific day.

3. If the salary isn't what you want, say that it came in a bit lower than you were hoping for, but you are incredibly excited about the opportunity and would love to see if there is any wiggle room.

Taking a day or two to contemplate an offer will not result in it being rescinded. Accepting a job is a big deal. Are there any outstanding questions about the compensation package and benefits? Do you understand how much paid time off you will have? Do you know how long the commute is and does that matter? Will you be expected to be in the office or mostly work from home? Just because you made it to the finish line doesn't mean you are done. Rethink how every aspect of your life will change and then decide if you want the job. And if the salary isn't where you want/need it to be, it's time to negotiate.

Negotiating

I could write an entire book about negotiating, but some masterful writers have already done that. I highly recommend *Ask for It*[1] by Linda Babcock and Sara Laschever and *Getting to Yes*[2] by Roger Fisher, William Ury, and Bruce Patton. Both destigmatize what for many is a scary notion, stating it doesn't have to be uncomfortable, contentious, or adversarial. Negotiating your salary for a new job should be as simple as negotiating with your significant other ("It's important for me to eat healthy this week because I have to fit into my dress for an event this weekend, so can we eat at a Mediterranean restaurant tonight and a Mexican restaurant after the event?") or your parents ("If I come home this weekend, can you come see me next week?"). *Ask for It* says to view negotiating as a tool to help bring about change when the desired result is dependent on the cooperation of others. Look at salary negotiations as creating a mutually beneficial agreement where everyone agrees about your value within the parameters of the role and budget.

First, review the amount of cash you need to support yourself and your family. If you didn't do this in chapter 13, now is the time. Make adjustments based on how your lifestyle may have changed. Once you've come up with a monthly number and are clear on the value you will bring to the role, you are ready to determine what each side's interests are. Let's start with you.

What is most important to you and in what order: salary, bonus, equity, benefits, 401K match, cash incentives (i.e., recognition/spot bonuses)? Do you need a certain amount of money to pay off student loans? Are you supporting parents with your new job?

Once you understand your own interests, ask questions about the entire compensation package to learn if your needs are aligned, but don't let those needs make you inflexible to options if they don't line up exactly. For example, you need $100,000 per year to survive but the company is offering you $80,000 plus a 25% bonus. It is not exactly what you wanted, but with the bonus, the compensation brings you to $100,000. If you're wondering how you'll survive on the $80,000 until the hoped-for bonus, you have two options: (1) ask for more salary, but it will be hard to bump the offer a full $20,000, or (2) ask the company for a $20,000+ signing bonus to bridge the gap until you receive that bonus the first year. Keep in mind signing bonuses are usually reserved for higher-level positions but it never hurts to ask. Note that signing bonuses are taxed at the highest rate and it's a one-time payment, so it is always better to get even a few thousand dollars more in your salary, which will also mean more money in your bonus if it's a percentage of your base pay.

It is also important to understand how equity plays into a compensation package. Equity is a complicated subject and during my time in

HR, I learned that most early career professionals don't understand the difference between restricted stock units (RSUs) and stock options, vesting schedules, when taxes need to be paid, and how equity can enhance your overall compensation package. I was like that, too, even when I became a VP at Viacom. I received an annual RSU grant and put the letter explaining the grant into a desk drawer. When I started working for a pre-IPO company (Roku) and was granted pre-IPO options, I educated myself about equity. Don't be afraid to ask questions about the equity being offered, and then research the value of that equity and how it may or may not enhance your overall compensation package.

My broker/investment advisor has told me horror stories about people who worked hard their whole lives and never understood investing and would never be able to retire. I am still not great at it but I'm learning. If you want to know more about investing, try *The Wall Street Journal: Complete Money and Investing Guidebook* by Dave Kansas.[3] It lays out a detailed explanation of the history of the stock market, Wall Street, investing, and the basics about different types of equity like mutual funds, bonds, and stock. If you want something more conversational so you understand how to invest and save for retirement, I recommend *More Than a Millionaire* by Randy Thurman,[4] CEO of Retirement Investment Advisors and a certified financial planner who works with high net worth individuals. His book is a comprehensive blend of investing fundamentals and strategies for increasing income while living a fulfilling life.

Once you identify your interests, *Ask For It* suggests determining if they could be perceived in a negative light and ruin your opportunity to negotiate a great deal or result in the company pulling back the offer. For example, did you tell the recruiter about an upcoming two-week family vacation and that you would like to start the new job after you come back? Or you want the company to cover the vacation with full pay even though you haven't accrued vacation time yet? Did you already tell the recruiter that you are fine with the salary range presented earlier in the process but now you want a figure outside that range? If you are going to spring any surprises in your upcoming negotiation, plan your strategy for them.

In talking to recruiters, here are their top six pet peeves when negotiating with a prospective candidate, any of which could cause the company to rescind their offer:

1. Candidates who try to negotiate every point in the compensation package. Don't create a list of changes you "must have" in the compensation package. This will leave the impression that you are demanding and this is your first real professional job! It will also suggest that you are ungrateful for the offer as presented if you want to change every aspect of it. If you must, pick one or two of the most important components to discuss.

2. Candidates who want a package that matches their friends' compensation packages. Every company handles compensation differently. Some put more emphasis on cash salary while others give a hefty bonus at the end of the year. Some companies include equity as part of "total rewards" and look at the offer holistically with the value of equity included. Others consider equity as "icing on the cake." Alissa from The Winford Group told me about a candidate who absolutely needed her gym membership covered. She didn't care that she'd be paid more than enough at the job to afford the membership on her own or that she would have equity for the first time to enhance her overall compensation. The candidate wouldn't budge, and the company rescinded its offer. The candidate also lost the recruiter's support to submit her for future job opportunities.

3. Candidates who send lengthy emails reiterating previous discussion points and providing detailed analysis of why candidate is correct. Once you have asked for an adjustment in the package, don't send a lengthy email with a detailed analysis defending your requests. If you are negotiating via email, be concise without too much detail. If you appear too greedy or uninformed, it could look like your priorities are in the wrong place.

4. Candidates who do not express enough interest in the role. You need to re-express your interest in the role at the beginning and end of each conversation and in every thank-you note and email or you may appear to be more interested in the money than the position and the company. Bob Hancock says that when a candidate is only focused on what they want, it feels as if they are using the offer to pressure other companies for a counteroffer and don't actually want the offered role.

5. Candidates who become combative. Some candidates treat a negotiation like a contest between them and the company. Don't do this! These are the people you are going to be working with! Just because you are a candidate for a job that negotiates vendor agreements doesn't mean you have to "win" in negotiating compensation. If you become adversarial, you will lose the job because you are giving the impression that you don't know how to effectively influence. I have heard of offers being pulled because of such negative vibes during negotiations.

6. Candidates who don't ask for something and then have a chip on their shoulder when they start the job. If you don't ask—and ask appropriately—you won't get what you want. That said, if you do ask and don't get what you want, decide if it's a deal-breaker. If you still accept the job, you can't walk in disgruntled because of what you didn't get. I remember in a first meeting with an employee how he told me he was offered so much more from Facebook and Google and that he was underpaid in his new role, which started a mere four weeks earlier. It definitely left a negative impression on me. You need to move forward with the best positive attitude and be committed to the role after you accept the job. Don't talk about how much of a pay cut you took, or other offers you turned down, or how much you "sacrificed" to get there.

How you handle negotiations will set the tone for how you enter the company. Nuff said!

Now you're ready to negotiate based on *your* interests but you still need to outline the company's interests. The best way to do that is to listen closely to what is being said during the interview process and in the offer being made and then ask questions. The company wants to hire you—that is the good news. But the hiring manager can only hire you within the confines of the company's compensation philosophy. Most companies have an interest in being perceived as paying employees fairly, attracting and retaining talented people, and motivating employees to help the company succeed while also supporting the company's overall business strategy. That means the company has a "total rewards" strategy that encompasses compensation, benefits, and short- and long-term incentive programs (like a 401K retirement program with an employer match, a sabbatical after so many years of work, and so on).

Discovering Company Compensation Philosophy

For most jobs, companies may offer cash, quarterly and/or annual bonuses, and/or equity as part of total cash compensation; and/or, in some circumstances, instant cash rewards such as spot bonuses. Some companies pay all cash while others offer a combination of other incentives. By understanding some basics about the company's interests, you will be a better negotiator. Here are a few questions to ask about the company's compensation philosophy:

1. Does the company's compensation philosophy lead, match, or lag the market? Companies will always end up in one of three compensation positions: leading, matching, or lagging the market. To answer this question, you first need to know how companies view "the market." For most, the "market" is determined from data that comes from employment survey companies such as Radford, Croner, and iMercer. They provide broad job data across multiple industries (e.g., data science jobs in all industries) or narrow data in a specific industry and size of company (e.g., all data science jobs in technology companies with fewer than 10,000 people). Depending on what information a company pays for and what companies are in the survey, salary ranges could be on target or very wrong. Also, companies don't always use the most recent surveys, so they are not always credible or keep up with the current economy. In a hot job market, salaries tend to rise because of competition, so candidates may have expectations that are much higher than the data. Also, survey data can be more regionally focused or city focused. An average job salary in the state of New York will most likely be different than what it is in New York City.

Most companies will look at market data in the city where a candidate will be working. A person who works in public relations in San Francisco will likely be paid more than a similar position in Oklahoma City. Some jobs, such as software engineer and data scientist roles, are so "hot" that they may be compensated similarly no matter where they are located. Companies have a ton of data on the market and what people should be paid for certain jobs. You can also find a lot of data online through Salary.com, Payscale.com, Monster.com, and Glassdoor. Knowing this data, you can ask smart questions to find out if a company is trying to hire you cheaply or its offer is low because the company's philosophy is to lag the market.

When I moved to Viacom, I was offered a higher title and, therefore, a higher salary than when I was at NBC. That said, I didn't ask the right questions and had no idea Viacom at the time was well known as lagging the market in salary and benefits compared to its competitors like Discovery and AMC and the major networks. A company may choose to lag the market because its culture is strong enough to attract and retain great talent, and this was true with Viacom back in the day, which for years was led by the immensely popular MTV and Nickelodeon. And since I was being offered a higher title and more money, I didn't even think to negotiate or check the market.

Roku, on the other hand, paid market rate in compensation and benefits for employees and new hires, which means it matched at least the 50th percentile of the range for a particular role. For example, if total compensation (cash, bonus) ranged from $50,000 for a less-experienced person to $100,000 for the most experienced, the offer may come in around $75,000.

Some companies like Netflix are well known to lead the market or pay higher salaries and/or benefits to attract and retain the best employees.

That doesn't mean they'll always pay top of the market; it means the company will pay more than 75% and sometimes over 100% of the market for the right candidate. But there can be a price to pay. At Netflix, it is well known that vacations are fine as long as you aren't stalling business. It is not uncommon to answer emails and calls at night, on weekends, and even on vacation. That's why you need to know what is most important to you because if culture, personal time, or something other than compensation is a priority and you understand a company's compensation philosophy, you will know if the offer is fair and will work for your lifestyle.

2. How are bonuses calculated? Incentive pay or "bonuses" may be offered by some companies to both motivate and compensate high performance in driving business results. Each company tailors their incentive pay program to fit the company's goals, and which can also be used to differentiate employees based on performance. You may be offered more cash and less incentive pay at one company and the exact opposite at another. Or, you may not be eligible for a bonus at all. If a bonus is offered, ask questions to understand how much of the bonus calculation is based on your performance versus the company's performance. You will also need to know what percentage of your overall pay the bonus will be based on. If your bonus is based on a percentage of your salary, you will want start with the highest salary possible.

3. Are there any other cash incentives such as spot bonuses or a 401K match? Some companies reward individuals for great work with spot bonuses. Managers and sometimes employees can send company-financed cash rewards to colleagues for their performance on certain projects, and employees can use those cash rewards for whatever they want. It is quite incentivizing and makes employees feel good when someone recognizes their hard work. But you can't control if or when you receive one. Better to focus on guaranteed money such as a 401K match where you control how much you put in, up to maximizing the match if the company offers one. These matches can seem like modest amounts, but it is free money and it adds up! Find out if your prospective employer offers such a 401K match as part of the overall package.

4. How do employees receive raises and promotions? The most common compensation system is "pay for performance" based on yearly evaluations and/or yearly base-pay increases. Two people performing the same job title may not be compensated the same amount because one is working at a higher level and outperforming the other. There is also market compensation where an employee is paid within the market range for the role based on their years of experience—although the employee won't see an increase until the market ranges change, their role expands, or they get promoted. Learn how to "move your pay up" before you start at the new company but be careful how you ask about it. If you focus too soon on how to get promoted, it may seem as if you don't want the job or the salary being offered or won't focus on the job you are being offered. You will want to ask this question generically; for example, "What would be considered 'exceeding expectations' in this role or working at a higher level?" or "Tell me about your annual review process and how merit increases are allocated?" These questions are better for the recruiter than the hiring manager. The recruiter is at the finish line of filling the role, and if you ask appropriately, the recruiter may not tell the hiring manager, who might misinterpret your intent.

5. What is the company's equity philosophy? Knowing who or what levels of a public organization receives equity will keep you from asking for something the company can't provide. Start by asking a simple question such as "Is there equity?" or "Who receives equity at the company?" If there is equity, follow up with, "Are there annual grants and how are those decided?" Every company that offers equity has an equity plan. They are long and comprehensive; few companies will provide a copy, so you most likely will need to negotiate without seeing it. If the company is pre-IPO (not public yet), it is good to know what happens to your equity if the company is sold or if the company goes public.

Knowing all aspects of the company's compensation and equity philosophies will help you understand what is behind the company's offer and whether you have wiggle room to ask for more.

Chapter 15 Summary

1. **Thank-you notes:** Use these notes to connect your experience and skills with the new role and remind potential employers what you would bring to the job.

2. **References:** Prepare your references to help them further the message of how your experiences (with examples) have prepared you for the new job.

3. **Review your interests:** Review what is most important to you in the negotiation—such as cash, bonus, equity, and title—so your focus is clear.

4. **Know the company's interests:** Gain as much knowledge as you can about the company, compensation, equity plans, and your role's market value to understand the company's interests.

16

A Classy Exit

"Don't cry because it's over. Smile because it happened."

—Dr. Seuss, children's author

You got the job! You accepted the offer! Now what? Breathe. Smile. And know the journey ahead of you is exciting. If you are currently working in a job that helped put you through school or pay your bills and had a great boss, express your gratefulness. If you had a bad experience, be gracious in your departure because your current role has led you to this new career or job. No matter which experiences you had, the exit path is the same, and it starts with giving your boss at least two weeks notice. Yes, notice. Simply tell your boss that you have received a job offer in your field of choice and that you have accepted, and your last day will be two weeks from the day you are having this conversation. This is an in-person conversation even if "in person" is on Zoom or a phone call. I have known people to email their bosses if their boss is traveling or there is so much bad blood that a conversation would lead to more personal trauma. That is understandable, but never stay in a job like that again!

I get it. I had one boss who never contacted me after I gave notice—not even on my last day. I had to leave her a voicemail. Then she tried to Facebook friend me a week after I was gone. Not kidding! I wanted to give another boss a piece of my mind and didn't, but wish I had. Another boss lied to me when trying to get me to stay after she received pressure from

Tip #16: Leave a company with dignity and show respect for your time there.

other senior leaders. Once I called my boss's boss to explain why I was leaving. What did it accomplish? Nothing, except make me look like a complainer. That boss is still employed in the same job and I regretted that conversation immediately after.

When I planned to leave Roku, I was in the middle of helping a leader with change management on a huge reorg and knew I had to finish it. I had been working on it for months and it would culminate in about three weeks. Could I have put in two weeks' notice? Yes, but that would have left all those people affected by the reorg in the hands of my boss who wasn't involved in the change management plan. That wouldn't have been fair to my boss or the leader who had to manage through the change or the employees affected. So, I stayed for three weeks, worked my butt off, and kept my departure quiet. Most people found out I was leaving during my last few days at the company and I left with my dignity intact—it was the right thing to do. The leader said to me, "How you leave a company says a lot about who you are." He was right. I believed in helping people and I wasn't going to leave that in someone else's hands.

Your attitude should look forward, not back. Don't burn bridges. You never know if your paths will cross again. Next we'll discuss how to leave a company with class.

Preparing for Your Departure

1. Written notice. If you are in an office type job, once you tell your boss you are departing, they will usually ask for something in writing with an end date. Your written communication should not include grievances. It should be positive and upbeat, thanking your boss for the opportunity to work at the company. For example:

Hi [boss's name],

As we discussed on the phone, this is my official notice of departure, with my last day being [date]. I have truly enjoyed my time here and my ability to contribute to such a stellar team/company. I wish [company name] nothing but the best and hope our professional paths cross again in the future.

Thank you,

[your name]

Even if you have issues with your boss or the company, write a professional note:

Hi [boss's name],

Please accept this email as my formal resignation. My last day will be [date]. I wish you the best of luck in the future.

Thanks,

[your name]

You should also send a goodbye email to vendors, external clients, and contacts. It should be simple and provide information about who to contact in your absence. For example:

Dear [name of contact]:

It has been a pleasure working with you for the past [number of] years. I have made the choice to depart [name of company]. Please contact [name of colleague/new contact] in the future. [his/her/their] contact information is below. I wish you all the best and hope our professional paths cross in the future.

[Add contact information for new contact.]

Best,

[your name]

Before you put in your notice, make a list of the people you want to say goodbye to in case you need to send them an email from your personal account.

2. Transition your work. Your goal is to leave the company and co-workers with all the information they need to carry on your responsibilities including a roadmap for where to find files. You may be leaving, but life continues for those you leave behind. Build a list of where files are stored and pass on historical and current information as quickly as possible to prevent deadlines from being missed or cross-functional partners from being negatively affected. Also, forward important emails to those who may need them. It's your job to make sure that business can seamlessly continue without you.

3. Train others. If you are still working when a new hire is made, especially in a service-industry job, or you will be handing your responsibilities over to a coworker, it is your job to train the person taking over your work on any nuances of the job.

4. Don't badmouth or gossip. Your job is to leave on a high note. You are the one leaving, so if you badmouth the company, you are badmouthing your colleagues' workplace. And while you may hate your boss, you will be seen as a "problem person" if you dump your grievances. If HR asks for an exit interview, leave out your emotions and opinions; just state the facts about how your boss or team or company may be failing in a constructive, actionable way. Any complaining will be dismissed as the gripes of a disgruntled—and—departing employee.

5. Don't say anything you can't back up with facts. Unfortunately, I have been privy to numerous terminations and voluntary departures. In exit interviews, I have often heard "hostile work environment" or "harassment" or "discrimination." If those are true, you should have brought them to HR's attention much earlier than on your way out the door. If you feared retaliation or not being heard and waited for your exit interview to bring them up, be willing to discuss the experiences that led to that level of accusation. Focus on providing dates, times, and facts without emotion. HR is obligated to investigate, and you may be saving your colleagues from the same.

6. Social media. If you left with class, don't ruin it on social media with a lengthy missive about how much you hated your old job, boss, colleagues, or company. As Frank Sinatra once said, "The best revenge is massive success." Go out and get it.

7. Draft an uplifting goodbye note. Your parting note should talk about how far the company/projects have come and how much enthusiasm you have for the company's future. Don't mention your new employer if writing from your work email but do include personal contact information. LinkedIn will inform everyone where you moved to if your settings allow, so focus on the past and present about the company you are leaving and not the future.

Take Time to Relax and Reflect

With that you have departed. Now what? I hope you have taken at least a few days off before starting your new job. No matter how great the experience at your last job, being able to decompress between jobs is critical to the success in your new role. It is even more critical if you are leaving a bad situation because you may experience PTSD-like symptoms in trying to move forward. Take the time to breathe, take walks, and reflect. Look back at all the things that went right in your last job and if there is anything you would change. And enjoy the moment—you just got your first professional adult job!

Chapter 16 Summary

1. **Resign:** Resign in person—or in this work-from-home era, via video call or at least verbally on a phone call—to your boss and then in written form so your exit can be processed.

2. **Transition work:** Create a roadmap of where to find key files and transfer emails to those who will be handling your work upon your departure.

3. **Train others:** Train anyone taking over your responsibilities on the nuances of the work so they can be successful in the role.

4. **Leave classy:** Leave with respect. Don't gossip, complain on social media, or create drama in your departure. Send a goodbye note that thanks the company for your time there.

5. **Take time to relax:** Take time before you start the next job to reflect upon your previous role and company—the good and bad. Determine how you want to enter the new job and what you may do differently.

17

The First 90 Days

"Starting a new job is always scary, or at least to me it's always scary. It's like the first day of school."

—Sean Maher, actor

Landing your first real professional job in your new career is just the beginning. The hiring manager believed in your ability to learn and bring value to the company; now you need to do just that. Recall what I wrote in chapter 5: The problem with trying to truly understand the (new) career is . . . you can't . . . "Since you haven't lived it yet, you will need to learn as much as you can about it and speak in ways that show you've done your homework and are serious about moving into that career." That preparation worked for the interview process, but now that you have arrived, the real work of learning and performing begins.

"Imposter syndrome" describes a condition when people feel like they are pretending to be someone they are not. If you believe you are an imposter, you won't be open to learning quickly because you will be too busy trying to prove what you do know so others won't discover you're an "imposter." But that strategy will likely backfire, making you appear arrogant or misinformed. You will lose an opportunity to learn the job from those who have been doing it for years. The reality is that you are not an imposter. You are new to the working world! You just need to learn the nuances of your working environment.

Tip #17: Keep an open mind while confidently learning about the role.

When I started my first HR job at Roku, I had never fired someone, never dealt with a compensation review, never orchestrated an org design or "reorg" with a comprehensive change management plan, and never formally coached internally. I had never worked in HR! Those six inches between my ears got the best of me as I worried whether I'd be "found out" because I was entering the company as a director in HR, a higher level than others who had been in HR for years. However, that lack of confidence helped me be vulnerable enough to know the value of listening, asking questions, learning expectations, and building relationships.

Listen

When starting any new job, the most important thing to do is listen. Co-Active Coaching trains coaches to understand there are three levels of listening.[1] Level One is when you are listening from inside your own head. While someone is talking, you are thinking about when you can interject your thoughts or that you forgot to defrost dinner or that you wish you had had a better night's sleep. Level One listening means you are only half listening—not really listening at all. In Level Two listening, "you are intensely focused on what the other person is saying. Nothing's distracting you. Thoughts about the past or the future don't intrude." You are fully with the person, hearing what they are saying so that your own thoughts don't enter your mind. Level Three listening is Level Two plus: "You hear more than just the words they're saying. You pick up on all sorts of other things—body language, the inflections and tone of their voice, their pauses and hesitations." You are listening from a more expansive perspective. Most of us are Level One or Level Two listeners. When listening on a new job, you want to be in Level Three as often as possible. From there it is easier to discern if someone is telling you the truth or holding back. You will pick up on whether someone is comfortable or uncomfortable talking to you.

If you are fortunate to receive feedback from your boss or colleagues within the first 90 days, listen closely to understand what it means as far as adjusting your work style to the culture. When I was scheduling introductions with stakeholders at Roku, I was super excited. I had secured my first HR job and was putting time on people's calendars to meet and say hello. Little did I know that two of the teams had been dealing with a major internal matter.

During one of those meet and greets, an employee in the legal department sat in front of me with her arms crossed while I was smiling, warm, and inviting, explaining that I was just trying to get to know key people. "Uh-huh," she said. I told her I was excited to be at Roku and looking to learn and understand the business and culture and would love any insight she could share. "Okay," she said. I then asked if she had been here long. "Yes." I kept trying to be lighthearted, but after ten minutes of one-word answers, I started talking about my family, San Jose, the weather—anything to fill up our time. When I met with two other people in legal and one in marketing, I had a similarly icy greeting, but was able to break through within the first ten minutes. Still, I knew something was up but couldn't figure out what.

The next day as I was walking past my boss's office, he said, "Hey, take it down a notch. You're scaring people." I was like, What!? I was happy, friendly, chatty. I was listening to people describe what was and wasn't working. How could I be scaring them? I went home that night concerned and thought about it overnight. Then it hit me: I was sending those invites as a director in HR! And in the meetings, I was filling dead air with small talk in my overly exuberant way. Most people only know HR as the place to go if you have a problem or are in trouble! And here I was, yapping away, and expecting people to open up to me as if I was just another colleague. From that day forward, I just walked the floor from cube to cube to say hello, and if someone wanted some time, I offered to meet with them right then or suggested putting time on my calendar. I also stopped filling the silence. When I stopped talking, others started!

While my boss's feedback wasn't exactly clear, I figured out what was wrong and how to adjust. Listening to feedback will help you course-correct quickly. And that employee who had her arms crossed? She found me in the cafeteria a few days later, apologized, and wanted to redo our meeting. Sure enough, she thought I was there to fire people. Years later, we laughed about it when she and another lawyer took me out for a farewell lunch before I left the company.

Ask Questions

Now that you know how to truly listen, ask smart questions. Enter the new company as a blank slate so you can learn. Forget the preconceived assumptions you had of your position and the company from the job description, your research, and interviews. Now is the time to be curious about every aspect of both your job and the business. I knew nothing about traditional HR when I entered Roku, but since I entered as a director and didn't want to be perceived as junior, I asked, "How do you terminate people HERE?" and "How do you view compensation HERE?" I remember asking one co-worker about the company's termination policy and her description felt cold and uncaring, which didn't feel authentic to me. When I asked my boss how *he* conducted terminations, I received a completely different answer, which was more about leaving the employee in the best way possible under the circumstances. This felt more authentic to who I wanted to be in such a difficult moment. Lesson learned: it is always good to ask more than one person how they handle sensitive issues.

In essence, what you do in those first 90 days is learn about the business before trying to make an impact. Ask questions about the company's products, how it generates revenue, how your work impacts the business, how the culture influences the business. Ask questions that help you understand the broader context of your work. As you learn about the business, you will undoubtedly learn about "problems." Every company has something held together by a paperclip and a Band-Aid that may have been working just fine for a long time. If you come in with an immediate solution of a binder clip without learning how and why the company addressed the problem as it did, you risk insulting every person who has been holding it together with the paperclip and Band-Aid. Therefore, seek to understand the history of the problem first, how the paperclip and Band-Aid came to be the solution, and whether they are still working. If they are, then tuck that binder clip away until it is needed. If they aren't, ask if anyone thought to use a binder clip. If someone tried that idea and failed, then you look like a curious person trying to learn the business. If no one had thought of it, you may turn out to be a hero. Either way, the right questions show that you respect the history and the people who brought the company to this point and are willing to collaborate on a solution without looking like a "savior."

Ultimately, understanding the business will allow you to be more effective, more quickly, and bring value quicker which will make you be seen as part of the team's success. Learning about the business never ends. No matter what level you are, stay apprised of trends, products, and competitors. Keep powerful questions in your toolkit to use when you need them. If you truly listen to the answers, each question will take you closer to the knowledge needed for success.

Understand the Expectations of the Role

My boss at Roku explained his expectations clearly: in the first 30 days, he wanted me to just listen and learn about the business. After 60 days, he expected me to be doing most of the job. In 90 days, he expected me to be fully performing my job. So, I took meet and greets in the first 30 days, asked questions, and listened. Sixty days later I was fully invested in all the problems in the departments I supported and had a lot of "firsts": first termination, first compensation review, first leave of absence, first investigation, first HR data analysis. By the time I hit 90 days, it felt like I had been in the role for years. I was coaching leaders to resolve problems and my stakeholders were happy.

When I first started as an HR business partner, I never asked about specific work expectations. And having no prior experience in such a role, I tried to be everything to everybody. As an innate people pleaser, I thought being involved in the most minutiae of problems while tackling the bigger org designs and leadership development matters was bringing value to the organization. It was, but it was killing me. By the time I left Roku, I was working nights, weekends, and mornings long before the sun came up. I thrived on the fast pace and feeling "needed," but the treadmill was wearing me down.

When I moved to Intuitive, I had a completely different experience. Now I had more than two years of HR business partner experience and knew the role. I was more confident in knowing what to expect, but I still didn't ask the most important questions to align the expectations of my stakeholders with my expectations of the role. That lack of understanding could have ruined an amazing opportunity. Since I thought I knew the role, I performed it the same way I did at Roku: trying to get an "early win." While taking meet and greets, listening intently, and offering what I felt was sage advice when asked, I noticed the reception was cool. I didn't realize that the way to bring value at Intuitive would be vastly different than how I brought value at Roku, despite the same title.

We all bring experiences from other jobs to new roles. Even though I had two years of HR experience, I needed to enter this role with a blank slate and learn not just about the business, but also how the role worked in this company. I went from working in a 1,200+-person company at Roku to one with 5,000+ people. I also went from entertainment, which is loosely regulated, to the highly regulated med-tech industry. And finally, I went from a "sports team" culture with little employee engagement to a company that treated its employees like family. One wasn't better than the other; they were simply different. And while the differences between companies may seem obvious, it is not always as obvious that the role you are doing will be different as well. That's why asking your stakeholders and your boss how they perceive your role is critical to success. Aligning with your stakeholders' expectations will inform you how to bring value to each stakeholder individually and ultimately the company.

Build Relationships

No matter what job you take, you will need to build relationships. Relationships aren't about having commonalities or laughing together. They are built from trust and can't be rushed. If you want a comprehensive guide on how to build trust, I recommend *Trust & Betrayal in the Workplace: Building Effective Relationships in Your Organization* by Dr. Dennis and Dr. Michelle Reina.[2] The Reinas go into detail on the three dimensions of building trust including Trust of Capability, Trust of Character, and Trust of Communication. This model equips people and teams with a shared understanding of how trust is built, how it's broken, and how it's rebuilt.

During the first 90 days of any job, you are a "newbie" and you are the "newbie" of all "newbies" since this is your first professional job! No one will expect you to have the answer to questions or know how to solve every problem. But every interaction, just like an interview, is your first impression. I have heard people immediately state after meeting a new employee, "I don't know about [new employee]." When probed further, I will hear comments like, "they talked the whole conversation," or "didn't listen or ask any questions," or "already said how to do something better without understanding the business." Breaking trust early in your new job without even realizing it could have a catastrophic impact on your future at the company. Understanding how trust is built before entering a new job will allow you to build relationships more quickly and set you up for long-term success.

Embrace the Change

No matter how excited you are about your first job, it is still a big change. For some, it is a jarring change. New people. New processes or lack of processes. New commute. New computer programs. New boss. New everything. Some people underestimate how challenging it is to start a new job where you don't know anyone and have to rebuild relationships and figure out how to bring value. Starting a new job will feel like the upside down bell curve below.

New Job Bell Curve

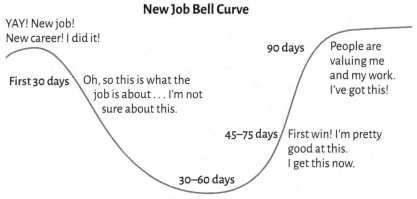

YAY! New job! New career! I did it!

First 30 days — Oh, so this is what the job is about . . . I'm not sure about this.

30–60 days

I should have never taken this job. I don't like this career after all. This is the biggest mistake of my life!

45–75 days — First win! I'm pretty good at this. I get this now.

90 days — People are valuing me and my work. I've got this!

This curve counsels that you need to give your transition some time. Starting a new job is overwhelming. Starting a new career is even crazier. And if you add in a new industry you've never interned in, that feeling of overwhelm can seem insurmountable. Just know that this is a major change and give yourself the gift of time to understand the new career completely before you decide whether you made the right choice.

If you are eating lunch at your desk alone, missing your college friends, feeling unsettled in the new culture, or scrambling to understand the company structure, you aren't alone. Most people need time to adjust to change. With every job I moved to, I sunk to the bottom quickly. But I also knew that everyone goes through this process. When I started at Intuitive, I promised myself to give it time, and if I still didn't like my job at the year mark, I would look for a new one. It took six months to settle in, and once I did, I was really happy to be there. Here are a few things I did that may help you:

1. **Be transparent.** I had an open and frank conversation with my boss about "not feeling connected" and "not fitting in." Your boss wants you to succeed. The hiring process and onboarding is long and arduous! My manager immediately went out and sought feedback, helped me adjust, and checked in on me during our weeklies to see how I was doing. Similar conversations with a few key colleagues also helped, as each one described their onboarding experience which was similar to mine.

2. **Let go of the old college life.** When college is over, it's over. It doesn't mean you can't have a great time on weeknights or weekends hanging out with your college friends. But your work week is mostly reserved for work. The quicker you accept that, the quicker you will move forward and adjust to the new reality.

3. **Look at the job through your values.** I thought about the positive aspects of my job in relation to my values. My boss was open, communicative, and supportive. And the employees really lived the company's values hanging on the wall. By

focusing on the areas that aligned with my values, I was able to look at the new job hardships as the natural challenges of change and I knew in the end I would be okay. And I was. And you will be, too!

New jobs are exciting, although the transition can be rough. But you have come this far; you found your first professional job. Now it is time to own it and give it everything you have to be successful. I believe in you. The journey is yours. . . .

Chapter 17 Summary

1. **Listen:** Speak less and listen more. Try to listen at a Level Two or Level Three to gain an understanding of the business, culture, and your role.

2. **Ask questions:** Be curious. Frame thoughts, ideas, and solutions in the form of a question and you can't go wrong.

3. **Understand expectations of the role:** Gain an understanding of how to bring value to the role.

4. **Build relationships:** Build trust through conversation, curiosity, and understanding.

5. **Embrace the change:** The first 90 days will be full of emotional ups and downs. Be open to discussing with your boss or a trusted colleague to get feedback on how to adjust more quickly.

Notes

Chapter 2

1. Co-Active Coaching Toolkit Values Clarification Exercise: https://learn.coactive.com/hubfs/2019%20Toolkit/Co-Active-Coaching-Toolkit-VALUES-CLARIFICATION-EXERCISE.pdf.

2. Values cards can be found online at Amazon.com by searching "values cards" or at www.easykickstart.com.

3. Davis Guggenheim, director. 2019. *Inside Bill's Brain: Decoding Bill Gates.* Netflix documentary.

Chapter 3

1. Bruce Tulgan. 2015. *Bridging the Soft Skills Gap: How to Teach the Missing Basics to Today's Young Talent.* Hoboken, NJ: Jossey-Bass.

2. World Economic Forum. May 2023. Future of Jobs Report. https://www.weforum.org/publications/the-future-of-jobs-report-2023/.

3. Megan Schaltegger. 2019. "Cadbury Is Hiring a Chocolate Taster and the Only Qualification Is 'A Passion for Confectionary.'" https://www.delish.com/food-news/a26553125/cadbury-hiring-taste-testers.

4. Orietta Gianjorio as told to Kelsey Kloss. 2021. "5 Secrets about Being a Professional Chocolate Taster." https://www.rd.com/food/fun/professional-chocolate-tasters.

Chapter 4

1. Dan Bova. 2023. "The 9 Most In-Demand Professional Certifications You Can Get Right Now." *Entrepreneur*, June 19. https://www.entrepreneur.com/starting-a-business/the-9-most-in-demand-professional-certifications-you-can/453592.

2. Katy Hopkins, Farran Powell, and Emma Kerr. 2020. "16 Tuition-Free Colleges." https://www.usnews.com/education/best-colleges /paying-for-college/slideshows/tuition-free-colleges.

3. Zack Friedman. 2019. "Here Are the Top 7 Websites for Free Online Education." *Forbes*, May 29. https://www.forbes.com/sites/zack-friedman/2019/05/29/free-online-education/?sh=3b81f10f342b.

4. Reid Hoffman and Ben Casnocha. 2012. *Start-Up of You*. New York: Crown.

5. Michael D. Watkins. 2013. *The First 90 Days*. Boston: Harvard Business Review Press.

Chapter 6

1. Ladders, Inc. 2018. "Ladders Updates Popular Recruiter Eye-Tracking Study with New Key Insights on How Job Seekers Can Improve Their Resumes." *PR Newswire*. https://www.prnewswire .com/news-releases/ladders-updates popular-recruiter-eye -tracking-study-with-new-key-insights-on-how-job seekers -can-improve-their-resumes-300744217.html.

2. Christina Zdanowicz and Amir Vera. 2018. "A Homeless Man Handing Out Resumes in Silicon Valley Gets More Than 200 Offers." https://www.cnn.com/2018/07/30/us/homeless-man -hands-out-resumes trnd/index.html; https://abc7.com/society /homeless-grad-lands-job-after handing-out-resumes-on-ca -street/4031443/.

3. Laura Italiano. 2018. "Homeless Man Hands Out Resumes, Gets Hundreds of Job Offers." https://nypost.com/2018/07/28 /homeless-man-hands-out-resumes-gets-hundreds-of-job-offers/; David Casarez. 2018. https://twitter.com/DavidCasarez17? ref_src =twsrc%5Etfw%7Ctwcamp%5Etweetembed%7Ctwterm%5E1032 013770724237312; https://abc7.com/society/homeless-grad-lands -job after-handing-out-resumes-on-ca-street/4031443.

Chapter 10

1. Eric Cheung. 2019. "A Woman Lied on Her Resume to Land a $185,000 a-Year Job. Now She's Going to Jail." CNN. https:// edition.cnn.com/2019/12/04/australia/australia-woman-jailed -fake resume-intl-hnk-scli/index.html

2. Floyd Norris. 2006. "RadioShack Chief Resigns After Lying." *New York Times*, February 21. https://www.nytimes.com/2006 /02/21/business/radioshack-chief-resigns after-lying.html.

3. Rachel Weiner. 2016. "Fox News Commentator Who Feds Say Faked a CIA Career Sentenced to 33 Months in Prison." *Washington Post*, July 15. https://www.washingtonpost.com/local/public-safety /fox-news-analyst still-wont-admit-he-was-not-in-cia/2016/07/14 /eb61b5e4-478e-11e6 bdb9-701687974517_story.html.

Chapter 12

1. Jeff Haden. 2017. "8 of 10 Self-Made Millionaires Were Not 'A' Students." *Inc.*, September 21. https://www.inc.com/jeff-haden/8 -of-10-self-made millionaires-were-not-a-students-instead-they -share-this-trait.html; John Haltiwanger. 2015. "Why C Students Usually End Up Being the Most Successful in Life." *Elite Daily*, May 19. https://www.elitedaily.com/money/c-students-are successful-in-life/1039028.

Chapter 13

1. *Merriam-Webster*, s.v. "culture (n.)." https://www.merriam-webster .com/dictionary/culture.

2. Netflix. https://jobs.netflix.com/culture.

3. Sissi Cao. 2018. "Jeff Bezos and Dwight Schrute Both Hate PowerPoint." *Observer*, April 19. https://observer.com/2018/04 /why-jeff-bezos-doesnt-allow-powerpoint-at-amazon-meetings/.

4. Amazon Bound. "The Essential Package." https://amazonbound
   .today/p/amazon-interview-course?gclid=EAIaIQobChMIyZeS34n
   C5QIVj8VkCh3O2AatEAMYASAAEgL NDvD_BwE.

5. Anwesha Majumder and Jessica Mason. 2024. National Partnership for Women & Families. https://nationalpartnership.org
   /wp-content/uploads/2023/02/americas-women-and-the-wage
   -gap.pdf

6. Amy Cuddy. 2015. *Presence: Bringing Your Boldest Self to Your Biggest Challenges*. New York: Little, Brown.

Chapter 15

1. Linda Babcock and Sara Laschever. 2008. *Ask For It*. New York:
   Bantam Dell.

2. Roger Fisher, William Urfa, and Bruce Patton. 2011. *Getting to Yes*,
   3rd ed. New York: Penguin.

3. Dave Kansas. 2005. *The Wall Street Journal: Complete Money and
   Investing Guidebook*. New York: Three Rivers Press.

4. Randy Thurman. 2018. *More Than a Millionaire*. Oklahoma City,
   OK: Master Key Publications.

Chapter 17

1. Co-Active Training Institute. 2018. "Listening." https://coactive
   .com/blog/listening/.

2. Dennis Reina and Michelle Reina. 2006. *Trust & Betrayal in the
   Workplace: Building Effective Relationships in Your Organization*.
   San Francisco: Berrett-Koehler.

About the Author

Marlo Lyons is a seasoned career strategist with more than two decades of experience empowering individuals to excel in their professional journeys. As a former TV news reporter, entertainment lawyer, and HR business partner, Marlo has navigated diverse industries and successfully transitioned her career multiple times.

Drawing from her own experiences and expertise, Marlo has dedicated herself to helping others achieve their career goals. Her first book, *Wanted → A New Career*, won the prestigious Eric Hoffer Award and became an Amazon bestseller. She is a consistent contributor to *Harvard Business Review, Ascend, Business Insider, Newsweek* and has appeared on podcasts around the world. As a globally certified career, executive, and team coach, she has worked with professionals worldwide and has provided strategic advice, career clarity guidance, leadership development, and career transition support. Marlo's unique blend of industry knowledge, personal insights, practical advice and coaching expertise makes her the foremost trusted authority on career development. Her passion for empowering emerging career professionals led her to write *Wanted → My First Career*, a comprehensive guide designed to equip college students and high school seniors with the tools they need to feel confident in choosing their first career and navigating the job market to land jobs that will bring them fulfillment.

For executive and career coaching and team coaching workshops, connect with Marlo at **www.marlolyonscoaching.com** or through social media:

Linked In	Instagram	TikTok

Index

Made in USA - Kendallville, IN
27307_9781737018131
12.04.2024 2130